GROWING TEACHERS:
Partnerships in Staff Development

GROWING TEACHERS:
Partnerships in Staff Development

Elizabeth Jones, Editor

National Association for the Education of Young Children
Washington, DC

National Association for the Education of Young Children
1509 16th Street, N.W.
Washington, DC 20036–1426

The National Association for the Education of Young Children (NAEYC) attempts through its publications programs to provide a forum for discussion of major issues and ideas in our field. We hope to provoke thought and promote professional growth. NAEYC wishes to thank the editor and authors, who donated much time and effort to develop this book as a contribution to our profession.

Library of Congress Catalog Card Number: 93–083115
ISBN Catalog Number: 0–935989–54–4
NAEYC #208

Editor: Polly Greenberg; *Book design and production:* Jack Zibulsky; *Cover photo:* Blakely Fetridge Bundy; *Copyediting:* Penny Atkins and Betty Nylund Barr

Printed in the United States of America

About the Authors

 **Elizabeth Jones,** editor, is a member of the faculty in human development at Pacific Oaks College, Pasadena, California, and resource team leader for Pasadena Community Partnerships. Her books include *The Play's the Thing: Teachers' Roles in Children's Play; Reading, Writing and Talking with Four, Five and Six Year Olds; Teaching Adults: An Active Learning Approach; On the Growing Edge: Notes by College Teachers Making Changes;* and *Dimensions of Teaching-Learning Environments.*

 **C. David Beers** is a member of the faculty in early childhood education at San Juan College, Farmington, New Mexico, and a CDA advisor.

 **Kathrin Greenough** is a visiting faculty member in early childhood education at the University of Alaska Southeast, Juneau, and a CDA advisor.

 **Margie Carter** is an early childhood consultant and video producer in Seattle, Washington, where she also teaches for Seattle community colleges and Pacific Oaks College outreach as adjunct faculty.

 **Joyce Robinson** is coordinator of the children's services department for Pasadena Unified School District in California.

 **Diedra Miller** is director of early childhood staff development programs at Pacific Oaks College and coordinates the Pasadena Community Partnerships.

 **Richard Cohen** is director of the research center at Pacific Oaks College and Children's Programs in Pasadena, California.

 **Gretchen Reynolds** is a member of the faculty in early childhood education at Algonquin College, Ottawa, Canada; a Pacific Oaks adjunct faculty member; and co-author of *The Play's the Thing*.

 **Jane Meade-Roberts** is a family day care provider and educational consultant in Salinas, California; she also teaches for Pacific Oaks College as adjunct faculty.

 **Joan Hillard** is superintendent of the Spreckels Union School District in Spreckels, California.

 **Maja Apelman** is an educational consultant in Boulder, Colorado, and co-author with Julie King of *Everyday Math: Explorations for Students, Teachers and Parents* (Heinemann, 1993).

 **Barbara Creaser** is an early childhood consultant in Canberra, Australia.

 **Lisa Poelle** is a child care consultant in San Jose, California.

ABOUT THE AUTHORS

Contents

Chapter 4
TEACHERS TALKING TO EACH OTHER: THE PASADENA PARTNERSHIP PROJECT
Elizabeth Jones, Joyce Robinson, Diedra Miller, Richard Cohen, and Gretchen Reynolds
54

Chapter 5
CHANGE MAKING IN A PRIMARY SCHOOL: SOLEDAD, CALIFORNIA
Jane Meade-Roberts, Elizabeth Jones, and Joan Hillard
74

Chapter 6
CO-CREATING PRIMARY CURRICULUM: BOULDER VALLEY SCHOOLS
Maja Apelman
90

Chapter 7
TEACHERS AS OBSERVERS OF PLAY: INVOLVING TEACHERS IN ACTION RESEARCH
Barbara Creaser
104

Chapter 8
I'LL VISIT YOUR CLASS, YOU VISIT MINE: EXPERIENCED TEACHERS AS MENTORS
Lisa Poelle
118

Chapter 9
LOOKING BACK: WHAT WE'VE LEARNED ABOUT PARTNERSHIPS
Elizabeth Jones
135

INFORMATION ABOUT NAEYC
151

G rowing teachers is different from training them. Oddly, we more often think about growing plants than about growing people. People, especially the young, are to be domesticated—trained as dogs and horses are—to make them reliable, responsible members of society. Plants, of course, can be trained, too, if we have decided on the precise direction we want them to take. We clip a little here, tie a little there, and are rewarded by just the shape we want to grace our pot or wall or formal garden.

An alternative to domestication is liberation (Freire, 1970). Teachers, like other people, need some of both. Many books have been written about teacher training, offering useful guidelines for improving practice toward specified outcomes. This book, in contrast, describes staff development activities that were open in design; philosophy and process were defined, but not outcomes. Teachers were expected to participate actively in the construction of knowledge about their work, making choices among options for growth.

Each of the stories told here involves a partnership between one or more early childhood programs—preschools, child care centers, public schools—and some other agency or individual working over time with teaching staff to facilitate their growth. Because facilitators were independent of the system that employed the teachers, they were free to encourage teachers' thinking rather than evaluate their performance. These storytellers have found this approach a particularly good fit in early childhood education. Here's why.

Introduction:
Growing Teachers

Elizabeth Jones

Teachers construct knowledge about teaching

People with power in educational systems—administrators, supervisors, trainers, consultants, professors, teachers—get their jobs because they are seen as experts—*people who know*. To most of those who know, it seems sensible to tell others what to do, whether those others are adults or children. And some kinds of knowledge—names for things, facts, rules for behavior—are indeed learned by memorizing what one is told by those who already know. Piaget calls this *social knowledge*; it is agreed upon by a particular society and taught directly to naive members of that society.

Piaget also has a lot to say about *logical knowledge*—the understandings or schemata that cannot be learned by rote but must be constructed by each knower in order to understand the relationships among things, events, and people. Young children construct logical knowledge by hands-on investigation, dramatic play, and discussion. Similarly, adults learn complex tasks and concepts by doing them and reflecting and dialoguing about them.

Jean Baker Miller (1976) has suggested that there are some tasks that can be learned, done, and evaluated with consistent precision. A bridge, for example, is designed and built according to agreed-upon technical knowledge; properly constructed, it will stand. Admittedly, an earthquake may crack it; but in the earthquake country where I live, builders now claim to be able to take even earthquakes into account in their designs.

There are other tasks, says Miller, that require continual on-the-spot decision making. They cannot be engineered because the interpersonal variables are too complex and the actors keep making unpredicted choices. Childrearing, she says, is one such task; teaching is another. An early childhood classroom is a continual series of earthquakes. Childrearing and teaching young children have traditionally been jobs that belong to women and are thus devalued in a logical-technical society that values prediction and control. Men (and some women) in education and psychology have, in fact, tried to redefine teaching in terms of engineering models such as behaviorism. Donmoyer (1981), discussing this history in education, proposes a growth model that is organic—not engineered—as more appropriate to the learning process. Like the facilitators in this book, he is interested in growing people rather than in training them.

Education needs theory, Kamii (1985a) has insisted, and her theory of choice is Piagetian constructivism—a complex model in which each human actor, in interaction with others, constructs his or her own continually shifting knowledge. A teacher working with many such human knowers can guide their learning only within a learning environment in which there is room for action and interaction and in which attention is paid to what is happening for each learner. In such a classroom the teacher becomes, not primarily someone who tells and corrects, but someone who watches; asks, "What happened? What did you notice?"; and reflects, "I noticed . . . " (Wasserman, 1990).

This book applies a constructivist model to staff development. Just as young children learn about their world by playing its scripts, teachers learn about teaching and learning by playing the *teaching* script, observing what happens, and discussing all of the possibilities with other teachers. In this process they come to see themselves as *people who know*— thereby, people capable of making appropriate choices for themselves and for children.

A View of How Adults (and Children) Learn

1. Under optimal conditions of safety and challenge, human beings are inherently curious, intrinsically motivated, self-directed learners (Rogers, 1969; Maslow, 1970).

2. Knowledge is constructed by the learner through action on the environment and interaction with peers (Piaget in Labinowicz, 1980, & Peterson, 1986).

3. The construction of knowledge involves narrative and socioemotional, as well as logical, connections. Knowing is embedded in collectively shared meanings and depends on validation in significant relationships (Erikson, 1950; Donaldson, 1978; Knowles, 1984; Noddings, 1984; Belenky et al., 1986; Jones, 1986; Egan, 1989).

4. Active, self-expressive learning is necessarily a social process; it should take place in, and contribute to, a democratic community of critical thinkers (Dewey, 1938, 1943).

5. Learning takes place in the context of social/political realities. In a diverse society, members of groups with unequal access to power often internalize oppression and fail to develop an effective voice. Education is never neutral; it can be designed to maintain or to change the status quo (Freire, 1970; Delpit, 1988; Derman-Sparks et al., 1989; Rose, 1989; Darder, 1991).

Choice making: Teachers take initiative

In this model the development of teacher *initiative* has priority. Young children in the stage of initiative (Erikson, 1950) are mastering learning-through-play, in which making choices and inventing one's own actions are the primary skills to be learned. In this stage children need facilitation of their spontaneous activity, not direct instruction. Similarly, where trust, autonomy, and a baseline of competence have been established, teachers are also intrinsically motivated to master learning-through-play, in which invention, action, and negotiation with peers lead to unpredicted but interesting and stimulating outcomes. Teachers will grow by making choices among teaching possibili-

Karen Lee Ensley

ties, observing children's responses, and reflecting through dialogue with facilitative and knowledgeable colleagues. Choice is a crucial component in enabling teachers to take responsibility for their own growth. Making choices is an empowering process.

What, then, about all of the early childhood program staff who "don't want to grow," who appear to lack both creativity and motivation? Again, young children offer a partial parallel. Some children have pressing needs that leave them with little energy for spontaneous play, but sometimes interesting materials and a helpful adult can entice these children into play, which helps them to move past anxiety toward competence. Many adults with complex lives have pressing needs that leave them with little energy to invest in their work beyond its minimum requirements, but some can be "hooked" in unexpected ways, especially if their personal priorities are acknowledged and a range of enticing choices is made available.

Teachers who aren't expected to take initiative probably won't. Teachers who are expected to may not, but the chances are better. Bennis has written (1976) of the human-relations or "truth/love" leadership model, which assumes

> that if we present enough valid data to people and develop a relationship of trust and affection and love, then change can come about. The theory relies on the idea that trust is a historical concept based on repeated interactions. That, if there's enough trust and enough truth, most changes can take place. (p. 88)

This model is based on faith in self-fulfilling prophecies—faith that ordinary teachers, viewed as interesting and competent by colleagues worthy of respect, will become more thoughtful about their work, will continue to seek input from others, and will thereby become increasingly empowered as critical thinkers and problem solvers.

Initiative or Power?

If you're responsible for a program, know what you want and have the authority and power to get what you want—go for it! Consider, however, these thoughts:

1. Teaching requires continual on-the-spot decision making. When you're not monitoring, teachers must make independent decisions that can never be entirely predictable.

2. In a rapidly changing society, traditional knowledge is never sufficient to cover all of the possibilities.

3. In a diverse society the knowledge base of any one culture is inadequate to answer the questions that come up when cultures meet.

4. Teachers who are supported in practicing autonomous problem solving will become more competent professionals than those who are expected to follow instructions.

5. Teachers accustomed to autonomy are more likely to question authority, and thus complicate administrators' lives, than teachers who are dependably obedient.

Note: Teachers and parents may find it instructive to construct a similar list substituting children *for* teachers.

When choice making isn't appropriate

The human-relations model works, says Bennis, but not often enough. Sometimes it's necessary to use the "power" model, in which the leader decides what she wants and gets it through the exercise of her power. The two models are complementary; it's important to choose the one more appropriate at a given time. In teaching young children we offer them many opportunities to make decisions for themselves, but there are times when they have to do something because we said so. In staff development there are comparable rules to be learned and followed; these represent the minimum standards for responsible teaching, the baseline of competence required of all staff. Some standards are determined by licensing agencies; others are set by program policy and enforced by administrators and supervisors. Compliance, not initiative, is the desired outcome. All classrooms are expected to be alike in their safety procedures; their attentiveness to children's health needs; and, in some programs, their implementation of a prescribed curriculum.

When teachers make choices some will grow more than others. They may become more different rather than more alike, directing their energies in varied ways, setting their own priorities, and developing a unique style of teaching as well as of professional growth. The organic development fostered in a growth model produces variety, not predictable sameness. It is more fruitful, more fun, and more risky.

Options in in-service education

Finding an appropriate balance between initiative and power is a challenge for both managers of programs and planners of in-service education for program staff. In programs functioning near the baseline of competence, staff development may require a *training* model, relying on expert information to reinforce program expectations. In contrast, programs with relatively stable, competent staff may find a *facilitation* model more effective in developing staff initiative toward high quality.

A staff development plan may emphasize training or facilitation, expert or collegial relationships, personal or impersonal relationships. It may rely on internal or external personnel for its implementation.

Options: Training or facilitation?

Teachers' preservice training, experience, and competence vary widely in preschool programs, both between centers and within them. Inexperienced, untrained teachers still in the survival stage (Katz, 1977) need straightforward training—social knowledge—that clarifies the expectations for their work and gives them recipes for getting started. Once teachers have developed a repertoire of group-management skills and activities that keep children interested, they are ready to construct their own knowledge through reflecting on practice, being challenged to grow, and making some choices about their rate and direction of growth. Their need is less for a trainer than for a facilitator—a colleague with whom to grow. In staff-development plans, training and facilitation balance each other. Programs with high staff turnover need a continuing training plan, while programs with relative stability need to explore a facilitation model.

Options: Expert or collegial?

Experts train; colleagues facilitate. Adults, like children, learn both through being told by those who already know and through discussion with peers who are in the process of constructing similar knowledge. The construction of knowledge, Piaget has suggested, takes place most effectively through interaction with peers, who can be argued with, not simply believed. An in-service plan may emphasize listening to experts or it may develop opportunities for staff to talk together. Persons who have expertise but choose to listen and question rather than give information directly may be able to build collegial relationships with teachers.

Literate learners may encounter significant others in print or visual media as well as face-to-face. Some books and films give how-to instructions; others tell stories that enable teachers to construct their own connections and understandings.

Options: Personal or impersonal contact?

Contact with experts and with peers can be personal or impersonal. Personal contact implies relationship and is usually face-to-face, although it is possible to build relationships through correspondence or interactive technology. Relationships are built on two-way interaction, although some writers and lecturers are able, through their personal style, to communicate an "as-if" experience of relationship to readers and listeners. Relationship building requires continuity over time.

Options: External or internal staff developers?

Some staff-development providers are employed within the system in which the teachers work and have line authority over them. Their relationships are necessarily different, in greater or lesser degree, from those of a trainer or consultant who comes from outside the system and has no power within it. The supervisor responsible for teacher performance is always at risk of being seen as evaluator if she observes and asks questions in classrooms.

* * *

The stories in this collection examine the work of resource people *external* to the system who have sought to develop *facilitative personal* relationships that build *collegiality* between themselves and teachers—usually, *experienced* teachers. We have chosen to call this role *storyteller* because of the importance of observation and reflection as facilitative behaviors and to contrast it with two roles we have observed in other situations, *fixer-upper* and *star*.

Fixer-uppers, stars, and storytellers

Fixer-uppers know what ought to be done and typically use suitable reinforcements to try to get it done. Fixer-uppers are most effective if they have power within the

---

Teachers as Learners

In *The Creation of Settings and the Future Societies* (1972), Sarason has articulated this principle in his description of a psychoeducational clinic:

"The clinic did not define its task in terms of service.... Our primary responsibility was to ourselves (the staff) in the sense that we had to learn new things. We were going to judge ourselves only secondarily by how helpful we were to others" (p. 116). "Our primary value concerns our need to help ourselves change and learn, for us to feel that we are growing in our understanding of where we have been, where we are, and what we are about, and that we are enjoying what we are doing" (p. 122).

"On those occasions when we gave this answer, the reactions varied, not surprisingly, from staring disbelief, to implicit accusations of narcissism and callousness, to a benevolence which seemed to view the answer as a kind of pious idealism which would not stand up in the real world. These reactions...reflect values and a way of thinking implicit in the creation of almost all settings.... I will use our schools as a case in point. Nobody would disagree with the statement that schools are primarily for the education of children.... What children should be taught, what experiences children should have, how much progress children should make—these questions reveal who is center stage. I have spent thousands of hours in schools and one of the first things I sensed was that the longer the person had been a teacher the less excited, or alive, or stimulated he seemed to be about his role. It was not that they were uninterested, or felt that what they were doing was unimportant, or that they were not being helpful to their students, but simply that being a teacher was on the boring side.... what would be inexplicable would be if things turned out otherwise, because schools are not created to foster the intellectual and professional growth of teachers. The assumption that teachers can create and maintain those conditions which make school learning and school living stimulating for children, without those same conditions existing for teachers, has no warrant in the history of man" (pp.123–124).

system as an administrator or supervisor or coercive power as a representative of a regulatory agency. Having made demands, the maker needs to be in a position to enforce them. Fixer-uppers have goals for the program and standards to be met, and they evaluate performance toward those standards. Ideally they are clear and direct in their communication of expectations.

Unless they are stars (see below) in their own right, fixer-uppers tend to rely on impersonal sources of expertise to justify their expectations; they cite published theories, written guidelines and standards, and marketed curricula. Such sources can be useful in depersonalizing any tension in relationships with staff. Rather than own responsibility for demanding something a teacher doesn't want to do, the administrator is free to express sympathy at a personal level while explaining that *they* (persons not present and not in the relationship with us) say that we have to. In many agencies and schools, this statement is not only strategic but true.

Stars are charismatic experts. They are very good at what they do and excited by the doing of it; their hope is to inspire others to do the same, through modeling and exhortation. They enjoy being on stage. Some stars do demonstration teaching; some do workshops or presentations in front of audiences. Typically, they are passionate in their concern for quality experiences for children, and they want others to catch their passion.

Stars' expertise may be shared either impersonally, as in lectures and one-shot demonstrations (in which some stars are very personal in style), or personally, over time, in the roles of model and mentor. Stars in master-teacher roles can be observed regularly by teachers-in-training in their classrooms, and the stars may be available to provide commentary on their own work and on others'. It is possible to be both star and administrator only in settings created to showcase one's work—usually small, private schools in which the star is teacher/director (and often founder).

Stars and fixer-uppers have a common priority: improving the program for children. They rely on expertise about early childhood education—their own or borrowed expertise—to influence teachers' performance.

Storytellers' priority is teacher growth. Storytellers have access to expertise—their own or borrowed—but they draw on it sparingly. Instead they look for the knowledge that teachers are already using and reflect it back to them, making teachers' own stories, rather than established

---

Learning To Distrust One's Own Thinking

Writing of autonomy as the aim of education, Kamii (1985b) describes her experience of asking primary grade children working in math workbooks "how they had arrived at a particular answer. Typically, they began erasing like mad, even when their answers were perfectly correct. Even in first grade many children already have learned to distrust their own thinking. Children who are discouraged from thinking autonomously will construct less knowledge than those who are mentally active and confident" (p. 46).

Similarly, many teachers who are asked questions assume that they must be doing something wrong.

1. Facilitators concentrate on strengths and ignore weaknesses. Fixer-uppers are in the habit of looking for weaknesses.

2. In actuality facilitators use selective reinforcement over time to shape teacher behavior in desired directions (Riley, 1980). These directions, however, are oriented toward teacher decision making, risk taking, divergent thinking, self-observation, reflection on practice, and speaking up, rather than toward implementation of any preselected curriculum or objectives. Facilitation implies commitment to adult learners as constructors of their own knowledge.

3. People with line authority in a system are responsible for ensuring that system objectives get met. This responsibility generally turns them into fixer-uppers rather than facilitators.

4. The people freest to facilitate rather than fix up are those external to the system. This way evaluation and facilitation don't get mixed up.

authority, the starting point for learning. The storyteller is both a collector and a reteller of others' stories.

The storyteller is a more experienced learner who chooses to be a learner with less experienced learners. While she cares a lot about children, in this role she focuses her caring on teachers. She is motivated by genuine interest in teachers as learners, which takes precedence over her own expectations for what should be happening with children. She believes that teachers who experience such support are likely, in turn, to provide it to the children they teach (see box on p. xvii). If she asks a teacher, "Why did you do that?" it's a real question, not a veiled criticism. She would like teachers to ask such real questions of children to support the development of logical thinking (see box on p. xviii). She's interested in the teacher's thinking and in stimulating dialogue in the teacher with herself as colleague and with a growing network of other teachers. To do so she necessarily commits to building a relationship over time; only stars and experts have the luxury of dropping in to do their thing.

Storytelling is most effective with a noncaptive audience, where teachers can choose whether or not to have their stories told and discussed. An external facilitator or a peer is most able to take on this role, working with interested teachers on a voluntary basis and counting on word-of-mouth to expand the network. It is difficult for an administrator to be a storyteller unless she is trusted to be nonjudgmental, and that may be a contradiction in terms; she is, in fact, the evaluator of teacher performance, and if she observes and asks questions in classrooms, evaluating must be what she's doing. Similarly, it is difficult for an administrator to be a star in her own territory; charisma isn't easily sustained from day to day. Administrators are expected, both by the staff they supervise and those who supervise them, to be fixer-uppers, responsible for articulating and enforcing standards.

Beginning teachers and teachers whose competence is in question do, in fact, need fixing up, through clear expectations and accountability for meeting those expectations. But different teachers need different challenges, just as different children do. An administrator working with experienced, competent teachers whose jobs are not at risk may experiment with "wearing different hats at different times, cultivating the behaviors suitable to each, making it clear when they are modeling and when they are monitoring" (Carter & Jones, 1990, p. 29).

Both system and personal characteristics will influence her ability to do so. Stability of staff and levels of authority are perhaps the most important system characteristics. To be free to facilitate, a director must have substantial autonomy. A middle manager in a bureaucracy is under too much system pressure. In any case, it may be more fruitful for administrators to find interesting ways to get teachers sharing ideas and resources—supporting each other as peers—or to arrange for external facilitation through some sort of trade or special funding. Outsiders challenge the administrator, relieve some of her isolation, and help her to think beyond her own program as well.

Personal characteristics of administrators who try a facilitation model, internal or external, must include relative freedom from anxiety about outcomes and an appreciation of teachers as independent thinkers. Storytelling is a process of helping teachers develop their own voices. Teachers who find their voices have lots to say and both the motivation and the energy to say it. They voice complaints and questions and new ideas. They may generate conflict rather than maintain a smooth status quo. These are not outcomes desired by a fixer-upper, who wants a model replicated, or by a star, who wants herself-as-model replicated. They are, however, desirable outcomes of a process whose goal is skill and confidence in divergent thinking.

Telling teachers their stories

Storytellers use their voices to reflect and develop teachers' voices. Stars often tell stories, too, but their stories are about themselves and the children they have worked with. Facilitator-storytellers observe and listen to teachers and to the children with whom those teachers work, and they collect stories to retell to teachers about *them*selves and *their* children.

Representation—in images and in spoken and written words—is a crucial tool used by human beings to make their experience real to themselves—to fix it in memory, reflect on it, and share it with others. Representation is primarily a social act. We come to know who we are and what we have experienced as others reflect our appearance, actions, and words back to us. Because self is a social creation (Mead, 1934), the degree of our self-esteem and the dimensions of our self-concept are shaped by all of the reactions of others to our growing selves.

Our conscious efforts to communicate to young children that "you are lovable and capable" are grounded in this view of development. Extended beyond childhood this view implies that adults, as well, need continuing reflections of themselves from others who care about them, admire them, and are committed to their growth. Teachers of young children facilitate their growth by providing them with time, space, and materials for play and language development, and by reflecting and representing back to them their play and their words. Facilitators of teacher development support teachers' growth by observing children in their classrooms, scribing their observations in words and pictures, and engaging in conversations in which teachers' and observers' perceptions are shared. In these interactions teachers experience a process equally appropriate for their interactions with children.

Stories can be retold in many ways—in conversation, on video, at in-services, or in a newsletter like this one, which goes regularly to all of the early childhood teachers in a school district:

Creating a Language-Rich Environment—Outdoors

Jefferson West Preschool

Mamie King, teacher
Georgina Villarino, teacher

Several children are busy with dolls and phones at a table.

Christina, handing phone to Mamie: It's your mom.

Mamie: Hello. How you doing? Did you pick up that hamburger meat for me? And what else did I tell you to get? Could you pick up some taco sauce for me—and lettuce and tomatoes? I'd really appreciate it.

Elizabeth, who has been skating, takes the phone.

Mamie: Elizabeth, I saw you at the roller rink last night. Were you roller skating? Who were you skating with—Melissa?

* * *

In the sand, three boys and a girl are making birthday cake, spreading sand carefully into pans.

Kein, to Georgina: It's your turn!

Georgina: OK, it's my turn to blow out the candles.

Eduardo, to Georgina: More cake?

Georgina: OK, vanilla. No more chocolate.

Georgina has been offered banana cake. "Estoy comiendo todo, ¡mira!" she says. "I finished already."

In this program the flow from Spanish to English to Spanish has the rhythm of a dance. Georgina speaks both Spanish and English. Mamie speaks English, but "They're teaching me Spanish," she explains, "and I make mistakes, so they aren't afraid to talk. Kein, who is Vietnamese, is *learning.* 'You're learning Spanish,' I said to him. 'Si,' he said."

"The whole thing," says Mamie, "is to get them to come out of their shells and use language—any language."

—From the ECE Community Partnerships Newsletter, November 16, 1992, Pacific Oaks College, Pasadena, California.

About the stories

In each of the partnerships described in this book, teachers have been encouraged to engage in reflection and dialogue through interactions with an external facilitator who has watched, listened, and retold teachers' stories to them. Facilitators have empowered teachers as communicators about their practice by devising ways for their stories to go somewhere—into print, onto video, or into in-service and conference presentations. Sharing teachers' stories builds their competence and self-esteem while passing their good ideas on to others. Teachers who recognize themselves as "people who know" are motivated to keep learning.

The partnerships described in this collection of stories provided staff development opportunities for teachers of children from infancy through age eight in half-day preschools, full-day child care centers, and elementary schools, in the western United States—rural and urban—and in Australia. All of the facilitators had experience in teaching young children, but none were employed by the schools with which they worked. Five of the facilitators were college instructors, one was employed part time as a vocational educator, and one was on staff at a teacher center. In the most complex model, a member of a community agency's consulting staff selected and supervised a group of experienced preschool teachers acting as mentors to inexperienced teachers in other preschools. These are the settings:

The rural Southwest (Head Start programs on the Navajo, Jicarilla Apache, and Ute Mountain Ute reservations in the Four Corners areas of New Mexico, Arizona, and Colorado): The partner was San Juan College in Farmington, New Mexico, providing advising for the Child Development Associate credential under a Head Start grant.

Southeast Alaska (Head Start programs in the small cities and native villages of this island coast): The University of Alaska—Southeast offered advising for the Child Development Associate credential in collaboration with Tlingit and Haida Indian Tribes under a Head Start grant.

The Seattle, Washington, metropolitan area: Independent child care programs joined a partnership offered by Renton Vocational-Technical Institute for child care vocational education funded by the state of Washington.

Pasadena, California (a mid-size city [population about 120,000] within the Los Angeles metropolitan area): Pacific Oaks College entered into a partnership, funded by the Ford Foundation, with the Children's Services Office of Pasadena Unified School District, working with teachers in the district's child care centers and state preschools.

Soledad, California (a small, largely Latino community in the agricultural Salinas Valley near Monterey): A consultant from a college faculty and a school resource teacher collaborated in staff development at the

---

But I'm an Administrator. Can I Be a Facilitator Too?

The answer to this question depends on

1. your trust in teachers' competence and initiative. Deep down, do you really believe they need you to improve them?

2. teachers' trust in your open-mindedness and support. If you have reservations about them, they'll know.

3. teachers' job security. Those who hire and fire can be trusted only so far.

district's primary school under a Title VII Bilingual Program grant.

Boulder, Colorado (a university community on the eastern slope of the Rockies, just north of Denver): A teacher center established at the University of Colorado with Ford Foundation support offered advising to elementary teachers in the Boulder Valley schools.

Adelaide and Darwin, Australia (the capital cities of two Australian states): In each a small, invited group of teachers shared classroom observations on a selected topic, working in Adelaide with two Kindergarten Union advisors and in Darwin with two faculty members at Northern Territory University.

Palo Alto, California: Independent preschool programs in the metropolitan area on the San Francisco peninsula joined a partnership initiated by the Children's Health Council, an independent community agency, with foundation support.

References

Belenky, M.F., Clinchy, B.M., Goldberger, N.R., & Tarule, J.M. (1986). *Women's ways of knowing: The development of self, voice and mind.* New York: Basic Books.

Bennis, W. (1976). *The unconscious conspiracy: Why leaders can't lead.* New York: AMACOM.

Carter, M., & Jones, E. (1990). The teacher as observer: The director as role model. *Child Care Information Exchange, 75*, 27–30.

Darder, A. (1991). *Culture and power in the classroom: A critical foundation for bicultural education.* New York: Bergin & Garvey.

Delpit, L. (1988). The silenced dialogue: Power and pedagogy in educating other people's children. *Harvard Educational Review, 58*(3), 280–298.

Derman-Sparks, L., & the ABC Task Force. (1989). *Anti-bias curriculum: Tools for empowering young children.* Washington, DC: NAEYC.

Dewey, J. (1938). *Experience and education.* New York: Macmillan.

Dewey, J. (1943). *The school and society.* New York: Macmillan. (original work published 1900)

Donaldson, M. (1978). *Children's minds.* Glasgow: Fontana/Collins.

Donmoyer, R. (1981). The politics of play: Ideological and organizational constraints on the inclusion of play experiences in the school curriculum. *Journal of Research and Development in Education, 14*(3), 11–18.

Egan, K. (1989). *Teaching as storytelling.* Chicago: University of Chicago Press.

Erikson, E. (1950). *Childhood and society.* New York: Norton.

Freire, P. (1970). *Pedagogy of the oppressed.* New York: Herder and Herder.

Jones, E. (1986). *Teaching adults.* Washington, DC: NAEYC.

Jones, E., & Reynolds, G. (1992). *The play's the thing: Teachers' roles in children's play.* New York: Teachers College Press.

Kamii, C. (1985a). Leading primary education toward excellence: Beyond worksheets and drill. *Young Children, 40*(6), 3–9.

Kamii, C. (1985b). *Young children reinvent arithmetic: Implications of Piaget's theory.* New York: Teachers College Press.

Katz, L.G. (1977). *Talks with teachers.* Washington, DC: NAEYC.

Knowles, M., & Associates (1984). *Andragogy in action: Applying modern principles of adult learning.* San Francisco: Jossey-Bass.

Labinowicz, E. (1980). *The Piaget primer: Thinking, learning, teaching.* Menlo Park, CA: Addison-Wesley.

Maslow, A. (1970). *Motivation and personality.* New York: Harper.

Mead, G.H. (1934). *Mind, self and society.* Chicago: University of Chicago Press.

Miller, J.B. (1976). *Toward a new psychology of women.* Boston: Beacon Press.

Noddings, N. (1984). *Caring: A feminine approach to ethics and moral education.* Berkeley, CA: University of California Press.

Peterson, R., & Felton-Collins, V. (1986). *The Piaget handbook for teachers and parents.* New York: Teachers College Press.

Riley, D. (1980). A method of human development consulting: The teaching of tools rather than answers. Unpublished master's thesis, Pacific Oaks College, Pasadena, CA. (Part of this thesis has been reprinted in Stine, S. [1983]. *Administration: A bedside guide.* Pasadena, CA: Pacific Oaks College.)

Rogers, C. (1969). *Freedom to learn.* Columbus, OH: Merrill.

Rose, M. (1989). *Lives on the boundary: The struggles and achievements of America's underprivileged.* New York: Free Press/Macmillan.

Sarason, S.B. (1972). *The creation of settings and the future societies.* San Francisco: Jossey-Bass.

Wasserman, S. (1990). *Serious players in the primary classroom.* New York: Teachers College Press.

Richard Ott

CH. 1—TELLING OUR STORIES: CDA PROCESS IN NATIVE AMERICAN HEAD START

F acilitation, by definition, is a voluntary relationship; it is done with, *not* done to, teachers. Of the partnerships whose stories are told in this book, some were voluntary from the outset; teachers individually chose to participate in collaborative inquiry about teaching (see chapters by Apelman, Creaser, & Poelle). In the majority of settings, however, the partnership was established with an employing agency—Head Start, a school district, or a school or child care center. Employers expected participating teachers to be improved in some way. It was the facilitators who insisted on adding elements of choice to the partnership design, with the assumption that members of captive audiences can be fixed but not grown.

David Beers and Kay Greenough, who tell their stories in the following chapters, worked with Native American Head Start teachers in geographically remote areas in the southwest and in Alaska. These teachers entered advisory relationships under the pressure of a change in national Head Start standards toward the Child Development Associate credential as a requirement for all programs. Their advisors were thus challenged to ask themselves, How can an essentially captive audience of teachers be empowered through the credentialing process? How can the competence of adults alienated from the educational system through oppressive past experiences be used as a base on which to build academic skills? How can an advisor from outside a program's culture help its teachers to grow? Their response is clear: only by becoming co-learners.

1

Chapter 1

Telling Our Stories: The CDA Process in Native American Head Start

C. David Beers

_____ **Notes From the Storyteller—A Personal Story*** _____

My name is Vivian Judith Loretto, but everyone calls me Judy. I have four children: Jeremy, Ivana, Elizabeth, and Allyssa. I work as a teacher in the Jicarilla Apache Head Start in Dulce, New Mexico.

I first came to Head Start as a very young parent. I dropped out of school in the tenth grade to raise my son. I jumped around from job to job in the community, doing a bit of everything. I was like...well,

_____

*Each chapter of this book begins with Notes From the Storyteller—*a narrative description collected as one of the "stories" created by the project discussed in the chapter. Here the storyteller is Judith Loretto, a Head Start teacher for whom David Beers was CDA advisor. This story was adapted from Judith Loretto's autobiography, written as part of her CDA portfolio and published in* Children Today, *March–April 1989.*

at that point in life you just don't know what you want; I was just bored with everything around me.

My Aunt Elizabeth invited me to enroll my son in Head Start where she worked. She encouraged me to keep him in the program even though he didn't like it much at first and I didn't understand what the whole Head Start thing was about. After awhile my son began to like the program, and I began to come in from time to time and just visit with the class.

One day I came up to Head Start to talk to my Aunt Elizabeth, and just by chance the speech therapist who comes there was looking for an aide. They asked me if I was interested in the job; they said they really liked the way I talked! So I gave it a try and I really enjoyed it.

I've been in Head Start for more than three years now, and it's changed my whole life! I was a speech therapist's aide for one year and a classroom teacher's aide for two years, and I just got my professional Child Development Associate (CDA) credential working with an advisor from San Juan College. I'm real proud of that!

It has been fun learning how to talk with kids and to understand what they are all about. Kids aren't just something you feed every day and play with every day—there is another side to children that I'd never really seen before I got involved with Head Start.

Preschool kids have definite stages of development they go through. Learning to be a Head Start teacher has taught me what a three-year-old can do and what a four-year-old can do. It's exciting to see what these kids can do! I try to reach out to parents to turn them on to what their kids can do. I say, "Hey, I am a young parent. I know what it's like. Come on in to Head Start. You might learn something like I did. I have four kids. You can do it too. Just give yourself a little more push is all. You can do it. You just gotta keep on trying."

Working on my CDA credential, I've found that I'm able to do college-level work in early childhood education courses offered here in Dulce by San Juan College. Going back to school was a real thrill. I never even came close to thinking I'd ever go back to school. I am amazed at all the information I've learned about the ways of teaching and talking with children since I started with Head Start. I believe that earning my CDA Credential is the first step in earning my master's degree in early childhood education. In fact, two of the Head Start teachers here who recently got their CDAs are planning to attend Fort Lewis College to get bachelor's degrees and elementary school teaching credentials.

My grandpa—he was always telling us to keep going, to hold our heads high. I had a lot of encouragement from my family. My mom is real proud. I have my CDA; my sister Amy (Loretto) got a CDA at the same time I did; my sister Irene (Lucero) is working on a CDA right now; and Mom's own sister Elizabeth (Muniz), our aunt, is working as the education coordinator at the Jicarilla Apache Head Start. It's very nice. All of us working here together and interacting with all the other Head Start staff. It's really neat when we all just sit down and brainstorm about what we're going to do to make this an even more successful program. We ask for volunteers for various projects, and we work well together because we want the best for the kids and the families here in Dulce.

But it is up to an individual as to what you do and what you gain. Like when Amy and I were working on our CDA portfolios, we encouraged each other. We stayed up twenty-four hours straight a few times. Once you get started writing and talking you just don't want to stop! It's a good life now. Being in Head Start has helped me in raising my own children. They are much more independent now. And it has given me a career. I'm much more independent now, too.

—*Judith Loretto*

The setting

Four Corners—where the states of Utah, Colorado, Arizona, and New Mexico come together—is sparsely populated high desert and mountains. The only large towns in the area are Durango, Colorado (population 20,000), the site of Fort Lewis College; and Farmington, New Mexico (population 30,000). San Juan College, the community college in Farmington, has a defined service area that includes the entire Four Corners region, extending for hundreds of miles in three states. To the west and south of Farmington is the large Navajo Indian Reservation, extending into New Mexico, Arizona, and Utah in an irregular rectangle about 100 by 200 miles, with a total population of 200,000, nearly half of all Native Americans in the nation. To the east of Farmington are small, traditional Hispanic communities and the Jicarilla Apache Reservation. To the north, in Colorado, are the Southern Ute and Ute Mountain Ute reservations.

San Juan County, where Farmington is located, is large, about 100 miles on each side; ethnically diverse, with a population 57% Anglo, 32% Native American, and 11% Hispanic; and relatively poor, with 25% of its population living in poverty. In 1980 only about 5% of the population had graduated from college. Nearly 50% of the nearby Navajo reservation live below the federally defined poverty level. In 1980 42% of Navajo families had children younger than six years of age, and in 1986 13% of people on the reservation were younger than four years of age. Preschool education is, therefore, a very high need on the Navajo reservation.

In this rugged area of topographic and climatic extremes, only 25% of roads on the reservation and a third of the roads in San Juan County are paved. Many Navajo families live in hogans distant from their nearest neighbors, on dirt roads that are impassable in snowy or muddy weather. Many of the 25 Head Start centers on the reservation are located in remote areas served by gravel roads. Few have telephones. Navajo is the first language of most children, and all of the Head Start programs are bilingual and bicultural.

In this rural, isolated area, some Head Start teachers have 20 or more years of experience, going back to the early days of Head Start. This characteristic of rural Native American Head Start is different from much national experience, in which child care workers turn over rapidly. Any program designed for teacher growth in this region is likely to have a long-term effect on the quality of its early childhood programs. To the degree that a program opens Head Start teachers' access to higher education opportunities, it is likely to have a significant effect on adult development as well.

The Child Development Associate Training and Credentialing Project described here was a partnership between San Juan College and three tribal Head

---

1. In bicultural settings, mutual learning is an essential part of effective training.

2. The facilitator who is a respectful learner can help build bridges between cultures.

3. The early childhood teacher who gains skill in bridge crossing can become a "cultural broker" for children, parents, and other teachers in her community.

> **1.** Teachers in isolated settings need training that supports their continuing reflection on practice and autonomous decision making.
>
> **2.** In the training of experienced teachers, it's important to assume that they know what they're doing and will grow through support in articulating what they do.
>
> **3.** New skills can be built on existing strengths; for example, writing can be built on oral storytelling.

Start programs with about 200 staff members: Navajo, Ute Mountain Ute, and Jicarilla Apache. The Ute Mountain Ute people live in the community of Towaoc, Colorado; the Jicarilla Apache, in Dulce, New Mexico. English is most children's first language among the Ute and Apache, although Head Start includes a bilingual, bicultural component. These communities have a centralized Head Start program; in Dulce there are four Head Start classrooms with an on-site director and education coordinator. In contrast, the large Navajo reservation is subdivided into five agencies, located at Crownpoint, Shiprock, Chinle, Tuba City, and Fort Defiance, each of which includes many chapters (small community centers serving a dispersed neighborhood). San Juan College worked with teachers in 25 chapters in three agencies, typically in a single Head Start classroom with an on-site staff of four: teacher, teacher assistant, cook, and bus driver (bus drivers also work in the classroom).

The Native American Head Start teacher acts as a kind of "cultural broker" between two distinct ways of life—ways of thinking, ways of talking, ways of handling issues that come up among children, and ways of relating to parents. She must be aware of both national standards and of how those standards relate to her own cultural background—to the history and tradition and language of the children and their families. To do so she must construct for herself, out of her observation and her life experience, a way of handling children that cannot be prescribed fully from a national point of view.

All of the factors described previously combine to make teacher training a formidable challenge. Between 1975, when CDA advising was first made available in this region, and 1987, when our project began, about 15 Native American Head Start staff became credentialed, a rate of approximately one per year. In the five years since this project began, about 100 Native Americans have been credentialed, and the majority have done so with the support of Native American CDA advisors, who were also trained through our project. Our major accomplishment is the adaptation of the national CDA process to meet the needs of this population.

Project funding began with two successive grants from the Head Start Bureau, U.S. Department of Health and Human Services, initiated by San Juan College in response to a request-for-proposals for CDA training in geographically remote areas. These grants supported (1) direct service in the form of individual CDA advising carrying college credit (with assessment fees paid for 20 candidates each year); (2) additional support to Native American CDA advisors and Head Start administrators, which took the form of an advisor-training course; and (3) development of CDA training materials based on

Richard Ott

our approach (see list of resources at the end of this chapter). This funding was supplemented by institutional support from San Juan College; by a grant from the New Mexico job training program; and by Navajo Head Start, which paid assessment fees for additional candidates. Reservation Head Start agencies have also contracted with the college for off-campus courses, using agency training funds to cover all costs, including books, and thus relieving candidates in these low-income communities of the worry about having to pay.

Who were the partners?

The partnership was established within the national standards provided by the CDA credential (Phillips, 1991). The CDA assessment process, for teachers of young children in preschools and child care centers, is a clearly defined but open framework, adaptable to local circum-

stances. The standards are defined in terms of six competency goals:

1. to establish and maintain a safe, healthy learning environment;

2. to advance physical and intellectual competency;

3. to support social and emotional development and provide positive guidance;

4. to establish positive and productive relationships with families;

5. to ensure a well-run, purposeful program responsive to participant needs; and

6. to maintain a commitment to professionalism.

Each goal is further subdivided [e.g., the first goal includes (a) safe, (b) healthy, and (c) learning environment] to create the 13 functional areas for which candidates are held accountable.

Several kinds of written documentation of competency are created in the process. One portion of the documentation, called a *portfolio*, is produced by the candidate. A CDA advisor produces documentation based on observations of the candidate at work and including recommendations for her continued professional growth. A local parent/community representative produces documentation that includes classroom observations and a set of responses to questionnaires by parents of children who are enrolled in the candidate's classroom. A representative from the National CDA Credentialing Program records observations from the classroom and from an intensive one-on-one interview with the candidate. The CDA representative also serves as leader of the local assessment team meeting, which also includes the advisor, the parent/community representative, and the candidate.

All of the documentation collected during the assessment process is thoroughly discussed at this meeting, and the team members analyze the records to make a judgment about the competence of the candidate. The four team members vote on the candidate's competence and, if all proper procedures have been followed, the national office issues the CDA credential to candidates who are deemed competent.*

At the time when the partnership began, the national Head Start office had proposed that the CDA credential become a requirement for lead teachers in classrooms receiving federal funds. The Head Start agencies in our region, which had few CDAs on staff, were thus eager to find a training plan that would enable competent teachers to become credentialed. San Juan College was eager to take on the challenge.

San Juan College

San Juan College is a public community college with an open-admissions policy; non–high school graduates may qualify for admission based on age and experience. San Juan College's 2,000 students mirror the ethnic diversity of the county. Classes are offered both on campus in Farmington and in communities more than 100 miles distant, in time frames to meet the needs of an adult working population. The early childhood education program enrolls some 100 students each year, most of them part time, and the college child development center is both a laboratory school for students and a child care site for children of students.

The early childhood education department was created in the fall of 1986, with

---

*Under CDA's new Council Model (1991), some changes in the assessment process are being implemented. With the substitution of a national standardized test for the requirement that each CDA candidate document her or his learning process in the form of a portfolio, the CDA credentialing process may, in my view, become less appropriate for the Native American candidates with whom we work. I have emphasized portfolio writing as the heart of the CDA advising approach.

one full-time faculty member. Its sequence of courses was built on the conceptual framework provided by the CDA credential, and a series of 1-unit field-experience classes designed to encourage the portfolio-writing process ties the work of the CDA advisor into the college's academic structure. When I joined the department as its second full-time faculty member in the fall of 1987, I took responsibility for direct advising of CDA candidates, for training Native American advisors, and for the preparation of training materials.

Native American Head Start

The Head Start programs needed to prepare for compliance with proposed national standards of credentialing. They were also committed to quality programs for the community's children and to the development of adult community leaders, including Head Start staff.

In these reservation communities working for Head Start is a good, stable, respected job, drawing on skills that people may have practiced as parents. Adults who enjoy and are intuitively competent with young children qualify for teacher assistant positions if they are regarded as responsible members of the community—a close-knit group of people, many of whom are related in a complex kinship network. Many staff members' first connection with Head Start was as parents; they were later recruited in acknowledgment of their potential as teachers.

The lead teacher in a center is more likely to be an older woman whose own children are in school or are grown, and in whom the community has confidence. Membership in the tribe is usually required and, in Navajo centers, where preference has been given to traditional people, fluency in the Navajo language is also required. Until the recently established national requirement of one CDA in each classroom, these programs have had no formal education requirement, although a high school diploma or GED has been an advantage.

Most of our first group of CDA candidates were lead teachers, all with a diploma or a GED and some college credit earned through Head Start training. They averaged 10 years of experience in Head Start, with a range of 5 to 25 years (as training has continued, a wider variety of staff, including assistants and several bus drivers, have become CDA candidates).

Native American Head Start staff are competent members of their communities. All have, as well, the bilingual/bicultural skills essential to their role as "cultural broker" between community life and mainstream America. They have not, however, necessarily experienced themselves as competent in their encounters with mainstream institutions, particularly schools. For many, English is a second language. Writing in English is a source of particular anxiety.

A partnership based on mutual respect

Native American adults have had much experience with being treated as disadvantaged. In an urban, technological society, rural subsistence living, in which spiritual values take precedence over material values, is statistically defined as substandard. In an English-speaking society, speakers of other languages are regarded as inferior. People who sustain a traditional culture are viewed as outsiders who can't make it in the mainstream. Even outside professionals who work in Native American communities may hold these views, regarding themselves as bringers of help to the unfortunate. Members of traditional groups may internalize these views, losing pride, self-confidence, and motivation for effective work.

In contrast, this partnership was built on a fundamental philosophy of respect and mutual learning. I am an Anglo professional, but I grew up in Farmington and have returned here by choice. My intimate childhood knowledge of the cultures of the region is a base for my adult respect for them, and this work is, for me, a coming home.

I regard Head Start teachers as fellow educators with whom my role, as college advisor, is to establish a collegial relationship. This means that power is shared between the advisor and the CDA candidate. What I can do is to help people validate what they already know and discover some things that will extend their skills. Concurrently, I am extending *my* knowledge and skills. Teacher development in a multi-

---

1. The external facilitator focuses on *adults* as learners. In her relationships with them, she demonstrates a style of respectful interaction also appropriate for adults with children.

2. Teaching-learning relationships are built in small groups over time.

3. Staff empowered through facilitative relationships may become, in turn, facilitators for their colleagues.

4. Among people traditionally lacking access to power, adult leadership development is a priority in ensuring their children's future.

> ## What Do You Do? Why Do You Do It That Way?
>
> By responding to questions like these, a teacher is able to describe and reflect upon her work with children. No teacher's story is *wrong*; it is an account of her current experience, communicated to an interested listener. If the listener takes responsibility for writing the story as it is told, it can be read and thought about again and again.

cultural setting such as ours requires a mutually respectful, two-way flow of information and influence. As advisor, I listen as well as lecture, learn as well as teach.

Staff development strategies

The strategies I have used in staff development center on preparation of the CDA portfolio, undertaken in the context of the Native American teacher as "cultural broker" in her community.

Portfolio writing

As described on page 6, several kinds of written documents—I like to think of them as *stories*, to use language closer to the daily lives of Native American teachers— are produced in the CDA assessment process. One portion of this documentation, the portfolio, is created by the candidate. It includes an autobiography, which serves as a resume of her personal and professional experience (Judith Loretto's story at the beginning of this chapter is taken from her autobiography). And it includes a program description of the candidate's preschool classroom, organized within the framework of CDA's 13 functional areas.

I have chosen to use the portfolio writing as the focus of my advisory work because it is, in fact, a storytelling proc-

ess, in which the candidate is invited to tell the story of her life as a person and as a Head Start teacher. Storytelling is a powerful tradition in Native American communities. The oral tradition is, for most teachers, a strength upon which we can build. It is also a style of interaction in which both candidates and advisors learn.

No person's story can be wrong; it simply *is*. It can, however, be told with more or less detail and clarity. By asking questions that encourage the teller to say more, the listener contributes to the quality of the story. "What do you do?" I ask the teacher. "Why do you do it that way? What lessons have you learned from your experience that will be of help in your classroom and possibly to other teachers as well?"

Although the portfolio must eventually be put in writing, we begin by talking. I encourage candidates to think of the portfolio as simply telling a story about the things they do as teachers. I ask them to put themselves into a frame of mind in which they observe themselves at work and reflect on what they observe, ask questions of themselves, ask questions of others—parents, elders, college teachers— and begin to integrate into their practice as educators the results of their own and others' reflection.

I might, for example, ask a candidate to tell what is happening in one of CDA's 13 functional areas. As she talks, I write down what she says. After a few minutes I simply hand the paper with the dictated words to the candidate and say, "Here's a first rough draft of a portfolio entry in that area. You've just told me what you do and why you do it that way. And that's what's required in a portfolio."

When you write a good portfolio entry in one of the 13 functional areas, you answer two fundamental questions: (1) What is happening in my classroom? and (2) Why do I do what I do? The candidate might ask, for example, "What happens in my classroom that affects the safety of the children?" I encourage her to answer this question in enough detail to enable another person to understand what she is doing in the classroom. The emphasis is on describing action. Then I ask her to explain why what she is doing is important to the children's development. In CDA jargon each portfolio entry must include both a description of what is happening and a "developmental statement" that shows that a candidate understands how her actions are related to the age and developmental stage of the children she works with (see examples on pp. 10 and 12).

The portfolio—even in the earliest, most awkward drafts—is a kind of window into the mind of the candidate. It documents what the candidate, an experienced educator, believes is important to make a part of the record. Because we are colleagues working together and learning from each other, as advisor my "First Rule" for reading draft portfolio entries is to make no corrections of spelling or grammar until invited to do so by the candidate. Instead, I simply ask questions about what the candidate intends to communicate and believes is important.

The storytelling that candidates are asked to do for the portfolio is much like the storytelling that happens in any group of people who care about each other and their work. Once the candidate is "given permission" to draw on this oral tradition, the writing becomes easier for her and grows in sophistication. She realizes that she can talk intelligently about her work with children in her classroom and, therefore, she can also write intelligently about it. This realization seems to be a breakthrough in the history of a successful candidate, the point at which she trans-

---

Functional Area: Communication   Entry #1

Story Time

I read stories that are familiar to the children in my class to develop their communication and language skills. As I read the stories, if the children know what will happen next, they will say the words with me. I often ask the children about the different events described in the stories and in what sequence they occurred.

When I observe the children playing out the different roles in the stories, I know they are communicating in a relaxed and comfortable atmosphere.

I read stories to stimulate the children's language and vocabulary. I know that it is important for them to have language stimulation so that they can learn to communicate their own thoughts and feelings.

—From the portfolio of Amy Loretto, CDA
Jicarilla Apache Head Start

forms herself from somebody who is afraid of the kind of writing that a portfolio requires to somebody who is eager to write her own how-to manual describing her learning process as a professional educator.

Teacher as "cultural broker"

The portfolio process provides the Native American Head Start teacher with the opportunity to create her own manual about how to be a good Head Start teacher, and I have been explicit in describing the task to teachers in this way. Such a manual or professional file incorporates elements from mainstream European American preschool education, along with elements from Native American traditions of childrearing and parent relationships. While developmental theory applies in some respects to children in all cultural groups, there are also ways in which Native American children are different from other children. What the teacher does and why she does it need to reflect both good standard practices from a national point of view and good practices from the Native American's own cultural point of view.

In the best portfolios produced by Native Americans, we see a great deal of discussion of culturally relevant materials in each of the 13 functional areas. This, in itself, is an extremely valuable resource for individual candidates, who begin to see the connection between their own cultural knowledge and their behavior as professionals in an early childhood setting. It's also important for the agencies that are responsible for creating a Head Start program that must meet national criteria as well as meet the needs of the parents in the communities in which they operate. I might also add that good portfolio entries are a very effective way of training the trainers, of advising the advisors, for they communicate information about culturally relevant materials not only to other Native

Richard Ott

Americans but also to advisors and other college staff from Anglo-American tradition. It's a two-way street, and we need this two-way street in order to be effective in our work.

The portfolio writing that I see at its best emphasizes this give-and-take between local conditions and national standards. It represents an intellectual task of the first order. This task, which all teachers face, is heightened in bicultural settings. If we are serious as citizens and educators about education's reflecting the needs of this pluralistic society, this task should be basic to the credentialing process. No standardized test can tap each teacher's unique knowledge.

Problems we have encountered

We are working with a bilingual, bicultural population few of whom have previous college work. Both the facts of their lives and the geographic setting make the

Hiding

One day, just before lunch, three little boys in my class began hiding in a room that was closed. No one is to be in the room because it has only one entrance and one exit.

I was reading a story to the children when I noticed that the three boys were missing from the group. When I finished the story, I sent the children down to the dining room for lunch. I walked toward the entrance to the room when I heard the three boys laughing. I entered the room and sat down by the exit. It was quiet.

I asked the children this question: "What would you do if a strong fire was burning right here?" The room is on the second floor. In the room are two windows.

One boy said, "I will climb out and jump to the tree!" He slowly crawled out from under the sleeping mats where he was hiding. He stood up and pointed out the window toward a tree that is about 20 feet away.

Another boy crawled out from under the sleeping mats, stood up, and said, "I'll bang the window out!"

I said, "The window has to stay closed. When a fire is burning, it wants more air to grow bigger. When the window is broken, more air comes in and the fire grows large, big. The fire can burn quickly, and the burn hurts you real bad! When the windows are closed, the fire stays small."

The third child came crawling out of his hiding place, holding his finger up in the air. The day before, he had accidentally burned his finger at home.

I said, "It hurts! Doesn't it?"

He said, "Yes!" and showed his burned finger to the other two boys.

I looked at him and said, "Would you like to get burned again?"

With a horrible remembrance expression on his face, he said, "No!"

I looked at each one and said, "If the fire alarm goes off, how am I going to find you if you are hiding?" They gave me no answer. They sat quietly.

I said, "I don't want you to get hurt. That is why I have explained to all of you that this room is closed."

They all were looking down. I said, pointing to them one by one, "Are you going to hide again in this room?"

They each said, "No!"

I said, "That's good. Now, let's all go down to the dining room."

We all walked down the stairs to the dining room. They each sat down at the table and began serving themselves.

*   *   *

This is an example of how I help three-, four-, and five-year-olds understand what can happen if they hide or get caught or lost in a dangerous place. They each spoke of their feelings during our conversation and learned why safety rules in the classroom are needed.

—*From the portfolio of Pauline Electric Warrior, CDA Jicarilla Apache Head Start* pursuit of a CDA credential difficult. Some candidates have no running water or central heat; subsistence activities, such as hauling water and firewood, take up a good deal of their time. Most live in small homes with a large number of people; they don't have much time or space for studying. Good Native American Head Start teachers are people who have many responsibilities in their communities; they are often busy on boards and committees, helping other members of their families and communities in various time-consuming undertakings. Family crises have priority over the CDA process.

When poor roads combine with poor weather, commuting to work and to college classes is difficult. Some people must travel 50 miles one way to get to classes held in Chinle, even when the college instructor has traveled 150 miles to offer the class off campus.

To obtain a CDA requires rigorous self-discipline, in the face of all of these obstacles, in a type of work that most of our candidates are unaccustomed to—writing in a foreign language. English is the second language for nearly all of the CDA candidates we serve, and their first languages are sustained by an oral tradition, not a written literature. Most candidates have had very uncomfortable experiences reading and writing in English. The psychological resistance to portfolio development and the lack of writing skill have been the largest barriers in our region to completion of the CDA credential.

Long-distance delivery of services across cultural barriers is an issue that must be faced by both candidates and college. Coordinating off-campus programs with the on-campus services of a college is never easy, even in a college committed to serving a rural, adult working population by providing alternate timeframes and class locations. We have needed to develop special systems in cooperation with on-campus people to handle the logistical details connected with registration, payment of fees, delivery of books, and the like. Getting a good program operational in the field carries a whole new set of challenges.

The facilitator role is one in which I believe strongly, based on my own extensive experience of implementing such a role as a CDA advisor. I have tried to teach this to others, especially to the group of Native American advisors described in the next section; however, as discussed elsewhere in this book, the role of expert is much more familiar to most trainers of teachers and is therefore easier for them to try to emulate (Hirshon, 1983). The candidates' relatively brief experience with me fails to outweigh all of their previous experience as students with teacher-experts, and they are already knowledgeable about the culture that I, as an advisor from mainstream culture, need to keep learning from the candidates with whom I work. Advisor training did enable Native American advisors to work successfully with CDA candidates; they did so, however, from their own perspective and not necessarily in the role of facilitative storyteller.

Teachers find their voices

The success of the first candidates to obtain the CDA credential had a powerful demonstration effect in the communities. Other Head Start staff also began to see themselves as persons who could obtain a CDA. We have encouraged those who complete the credential to take professional responsibility for helping other people; they have done so both informally—as friends, relatives, and colleagues—and formally, in the role of CDA advisor.

Of the 16 advisors now working with candidates in the region, 13 are Native American. Because isolated Native American Head Start projects had previously found it difficult to obtain consistent, competent CDA advisor support from distant organizations, these advisors are a significant resource pool. Most were trained in a course, Introduction to CDA Advising, offered by San Juan College in cooperation with the Navajo Division of Child Development. In the fall of 1988, some 25 persons, all CDAs themselves, enrolled in this class—15 from the Shiprock Agency, who were able to commute to the campus, and 10 from the Chinle Agency 150 miles southwest of the campus, who attended a section of the class taught on site at the agency. The instructor, myself, was an experienced CDA advisor and representative.

Coursework was timed to match the sequence of tasks involved in CDA advising. The class required that each CDA advisor enrolled (1) be working with one CDA candidate during the current semester; (2) be available for three observations and feedback sessions, spaced three weeks apart, in candidates' classrooms; and (3) be available for academic class meetings on five Fridays for three hours each and for two all-day Thursday class meetings near the beginning and the end of the semester. It was necessary that the advisor's employer (usually the Head Start agency) grant release time for observations and for class attendance.

In addition to the CDA materials for advisors and candidates, reading material for this class included *How to Talk So Kids Will Listen and Listen So Kids Will Talk* (Faver & Mazlish, 1982; we suggested rewording the title of the book to read "How to Talk So CDA Candidates Will Listen and How to Listen So CDA Candidates Will Talk") and *Sometimes a Shining Moment: The Foxfire Experience* (Wiggington, 1986), which provides a detailed guide showing how people discover how to write about their own experiences.* Advisors received ongoing support by interacting with each other and with the instructor, and they helped to prepare training materials for dissemination to other candidates and advisors. The final product for each student in the class was his or her own manual on "How to Do CDA Advising," including periodic status reports on each of the individual candidates.

This book, which I have found very helpful in developing training materials, did not "catch on" with Native Americans.

---

1. In a literate society, words-in-print have power to confirm and influence knowledge.

2. Those of us who are outsiders in mainstream America are unaccustomed to seeing *our* words in print.

3. Training materials typically come in the words of "the other"—an expert unknown to *us*.

4. A facilitator who records *our* words begins the creation of a "popular library" (Freire & Macedo, 1987, p. 43) of knowledge generated in *our* early childhood community.

5. For adults, as for children, opportunities to read one's own words serve as powerful motivators for the continuing development of competence in writing and reading.

1. Partnerships in staff development must be adaptable to the communities they serve.

2. A college can be an effective partner if it is open to change in timeframes, location of classes, student services procedures, design of classes, instructional modes, and instructors' degree of autonomy.

3. A college effectively serving previously underserved populations will be significantly changed by the encounter. Effective learning across cultures is a two-way dialogue in which prior assumptions are challenged and both parties are changed (Gonzales-Mena, 1993).

Other final products in both Chinle and Shiprock were workshops aimed at CDA candidates and their parent community representatives. Two large workshops, designed and presented by the advisors as a group, formed the basis of a series of smaller workshops given by individual advisors for parent community representatives and candidates in local Head Start centers. The bilingual approach used in the classroom with children was also used in the adult workshops—with great effectiveness. In our experience the proposed national requirement of a CDA in each classroom is workable in Native American communities and provides support for local training activities. It is an example of a national policy that makes sense at the local level.

During this project we realized the possibility of pulling together materials prepared by individual Native Americans, drawn from their portfolio writing, to be combined and edited into a how-to-do-it manual for Native American Head Start programs. We encouraged candidates to include sufficient detail so that a teacher in one classroom could read another teacher's portfolio entry and see how it might be applied in her own setting. In the best of these portfolios, there is a quality of mind and heart that incorporates a Native American orientation. In all of the training materi-

als produced by San Juan College (see list at the end of this chapter), the writing of Native American teachers provides much of the text, further affirming their knowledge of competence and extending it beyond the isolated settings in which they work to the larger professional community.

For local Head Start administrators, a teacher who can function effectively in the bilingual classroom is of primary importance. A competent portfolio serves to reassure Native American Head Start managers that the CDA process is one that is relevant to their own setting as well as to national standards. The portfolio also represents important documentation that can be used in making decisions about promotion to jobs beyond teaching in the classroom, most of which require report writing and literacy skills. We have seen examples of Head Start teachers being promoted into supervisory and training jobs shortly after getting the CDA credential. The work that they put into their portfolios was surely one of the elements strongly considered by the agency in making these promotions. A good portfolio thus serves not only the candidate's career goals but also the agency's goals of identifying capable people and putting them into jobs where they can broaden their impact.

Integration of the CDA credential process into the early childhood education program at San Juan College provides a foundation for candidates to continue a college education, if they so choose. Completion of the CDA-based course sequence qualifies persons for a one-year certificate in early childhood education. Completion of additional general education requirements can lead to the Associate of Arts degree in early childhood education from San Juan College. Several people credentialed in our program are now working toward this degree, with the intention of moving toward a bachelor's degree and public school teaching.

What was taught and learned

In this partnership we have found it possible to translate the givens of a national model into a culturally relevant "storytelling" approach that empowers adult learners whose previous educational experiences have typically been negative. The process of developing a portfolio provides the CDA candidate with the opportunity to reflect upon her experience as a Head Start teacher, to identify her strengths and weaknesses compared to national standards, to take steps to correct weaknesses and build upon strengths, and to document for herself and for others the lessons she has learned from this self-reflective process. The candidate becomes an observer of her own behavior and a teller of her own story.

As with many complex self-development tasks, this process takes time and consistent practice to develop. The Native American candidates with whom we work report that the process of developing a portfolio starts painfully and slowly, with a great deal of anxiety and anguish over the writing task itself. As the candidate becomes more familiar with the task of looking at her own behavior and telling her own story, she finds that the writing

becomes easier and easier. We have noticed as advisors that typically the quantity as well as the quality of the writing and thinking gets remarkably better over the period of months spent working with the candidate.

This approach to portfolio writing is a technique for promoting adult literacy. Most of the candidates we serve have been high school dropouts or do not consider themselves skillful at European-American intellectual tasks such as writing in a foreign language (English). They are usually afraid of writing when they begin the portfolio. But as they realize that they can write well about something they know and care deeply about—Head Start teaching—they find that their writing skills develop and blossom quickly and powerfully. This is a phenomenon that has also been documented with young children in the development of language skills (Ashton-Warner, 1983; Graves, 1983; Johnson, 1987).

Part of the purpose of portfolio development is to build the teacher's confidence and make a public record of her skill. Teachers who have had the experience of writing good portfolios become teachers with increased willingness to have children draw pictures and dictate stories. Children's language development and growth in literacy increase as teachers become more comfortable with their own writing. We find that we are responding to the national CDA's program goal—to "improve the candidate's skills in ways that are satisfying for themselves and beneficial for children" (Phillips, 1991).

Young children's growth in language and literacy is accompanied and supported by their growth in drawing and building; the different modes of representation of experience complement each other (Dyson, 1989). Working with adults we have encouraged the inclusion in their portfolios of drawing, photographs, and other kinds of artwork. In the Native American communities that we serve, there are many significant artists in rug weaving, basket making, beadwork, and other traditional crafts. Some of these artists are also Head Start teachers. Their artistic ability is evident as they work with children and as they produce their portfolios, and we encourage and support it.

The Head Start professional who is motivated to examine her own behavior is in a position to continue that behavior once she has developed skill in it, past the time involved in the credentialing process itself. We have grown to emphasize portfolio writing so heavily because we realize that the interaction of the candidate with the CDA credentialing process is a fairly short-term affair. For a person who makes Head Start teaching a career, a very important goal of this process is to give the teacher some skills in looking at her own behavior against some standards that represent good practices on a national basis, and to give that person a good deal of practice in using these skills so that by the time credentialing is finished, she is truly comfortable in doing so.

As we see it, it's not as important that she continue to write, although many do so, as that she internalize the mental discipline of observing and reflecting on her own behavior in order to talk through and think through issues such as these: "Is what I'm doing here good for children? Do children grow and prosper from this?" She can then modify her own behavior based on the feedback she provides herself. In a setting in which each person who gets a CDA credential is likely to have a long career in early childhood education, a long-term commitment to self-reflection is of great importance.

Our experience indicates that Head Start is good not only for children but for the adults who teach those children, and —significantly—it is good for the adults who teach the teachers. In this sense the design of Head Start and the design of the CDA process are superb models on which to base our work. Given our experience, we would say that not only is this a good way to conduct education, it's a good way to conduct human life.

In taking stories seriously we are in good company. The business management book that has sold more copies than any other is titled *In Search of Excellence: Lessons Learned from America's Best-Run Companies*, (Peters & Waterman, 1975). One section of its sequel (Peters & Austin, 1985) is titled "The Coach as Storyteller," and these words are found there:

> Nothing reveals more of what a company really cares about than its stories and legends—i.e., its folk wisdom . . . leaders use stories to persuade, symbolize and guide day-to-day actions; there's simply nothing better than a story to tell people what they really want to know about "how things work around here," or to illustrate the right thing to do in a given situation. They can lend believability and impact to a company's philosophy (in fact, they are almost the only routes to believability)— they will highlight, with lightning speed, any gaps between what a company says its values are and what it actually holds dear. That is, you are simply as good or as bad, as consistent or inconsistent, as your stories. You can like that or not. You can ignore it or manage it and guide it. But it is a fact. (p. 334)

* * *

I will tell you something about
stories,
[he said]
They aren't just entertainment.
Don't be fooled,
They are all we have, you see,
all we have to fight off
illness and death.
What She Said:
The only cure
I know
is a good ceremony,
that's what she said.

These are among the opening words from *Ceremony*, a novel by Leslie Marmon Silko (1977), a Native American author from New Mexico. We have been exploring a new way to educate Native American Head Start teachers that draws on their cultural traditions of storytelling and ceremony. Unlike trainers coming from the expert model, we have chosen to listen to stories more than to tell them. We have listened to teachers' words, watched them at work, scribed their words, photographed their actions, and engaged with them in reflection and dialogue.

We have asked, Could ancient storytelling traditions be adapted to the modern requirements of portfolio writing? Could a respectable portfolio be constructed as a series of stories that reveal the CDA candidate's development as an early childhood educator? If these stories were well and truly told, would a CDA credential be awarded? Would this be a fitting "ceremony"? We didn't know the answers to these questions when we began, but we have found them to be a resounding "Yes."

For further information

Beers, C.D. (1989). Storytelling and Native American CDA's. *Children Today, 18*(2), 24–25.

Beers, C.D., & Ott, R. (1991). *Well-told stories* [videotape]. Farmington, NM: San Juan College.

Beers, C.D., Ott, R., & Dunn, P. (1993). *Sharing stories: Active learning for adults and children.* Farmington, NM: The Child Development Training Consortium. "An introduction to the tool kit" (7 publications and 7 videos)

Beers, C.D., Ott, R., & others. (1990). *Stories that teach: Lessons learned from Native American Head Start classrooms about CDA training.* Farmington, NM: San Juan College.

Loretto, J. (1989). A Native American CDA: My personal story. *Children Today, 18*(2), 26–27.

Other suggested readings

Agee, J., & Evans, W. (1973). *Let us now praise famous men.* Boston: Houghton Mifflin.

Ashton-Warner, S. (1963). *Teacher.* New York: Simon and Schuster.

Bateson, M.C. (1990). *Composing a life.* New York: Penguin.

Bingham, S. (Ed.). (1982). *Between sacred mountains.* Chinle, AZ: Rock Point Community School, Navajo Nation.

Coles, R. (1990). *The call of stories.* Boston: Houghton Mifflin.

Doig, I. (1978). *This house of sky: Landscapes of a western mind.* New York: Harcourt Brace Jovanovich.

Gardner, H. (1989). *To open minds: Chinese clues to the dilemma of contemporary education.* New York: Basic Books.

Graves, D.H. (1990). *Discover your own literacy.* Portsmouth, NH: Heinemann.

Iverson, P. (1983). *The Navajo nation.* Albuquerque: University of New Mexico Press.

Jones, E., & Reynolds, G. (1992). *The play's the thing: Teachers' roles in children's play.* New York: Teachers College Press.

Jones, E. (1986). *Teaching adults: An active learning approach.* Washington, DC: NAEYC.

Momaday, N.S. (1968). *House made of dawn.* New York: Harper and Row.

Nelson, R. (1989). *The island within.* San Francisco: North Point Press.

Schorr, L.B. (1988). *Within our reach: Breaking the cycle of disadvantage.* New York: Doubleday.

Silko, L.M. (1981). *Storyteller.* New York: Seaver.

Trimble, S. (Ed.). (1988). *Our voices, our land.* Flagstaff, AZ: Northland Press.

Wurman, R.S. (1989). *Information anxiety.* New York: Doubleday.

Additional sources on Native American culture and issues

Labriola National American Indian Data Center, Hayden Library, Arizona State University, Tempe, AZ 85287, (602) 965–6490.

Sturtevant, W.C., & others. (Eds.). (1983 to date). *Handbook of North American Indians.* (20 vols.). Washington, DC: Smithsonian Institution/U.S. Government Printing Office.

References

Ashton-Warner, S. (1983). *Teacher.* New York: Simon & Schuster.

Dyson, A.H. (1989). *Multiple worlds of child writers: Friends learning to write.* New York: Teachers College Press.

Faver, A., & Mazlish, E. (1982). *How to talk so kids will listen and listen so kids will talk.* New York: Avon Books.

Freire, P., & Macedo, D. (1987). *Literacy: Reading the word and the world.* South Hadley, MA: Bergin & Garvey.

Graves, D. (1983). *Writing: Teachers and children at work.* Portsmouth, NH: Heinemann.

Gonzales-Mena, J. (1993). *Multicultural issues in child care.* Mountain View, CA: Mayfield.

Hirshon, S. (1983). *And also teach them to read.* Westport, CT: Lawrence Hill.

Johnson, K. (1987). *Doing words.* Boston: Houghton Mifflin.

Peters, T., & Austin, N. (1985). *A passion for excellence: The leadership difference.* New York: Random House.

Peters, T., & Waterman, R. (1975). *In search of excellence: Lessons learned from America's best-run companies.* Glencoe, IL: Free Press.

Phillips, C.B. (Ed.). (1991). *Essentials for Child Development Associates working with young children.* Washington, DC: Council for Early Childhood Professional Recognition.

Silko, L.M. (1977). *Ceremony.* New York: Viking Penguin.

Wiggington, E. (1986). *Sometimes a shining moment: The Foxfire experience.* New York: Anchor Books.

To contact the author, write C. David Beers, San Juan College, 4601 College Blvd., Farmington, NM 87402.

21

Chapter 2

Moving Out of Silence: The CDA Process With Alaska Native Teachers

Kathrin Greenough

_____ **Notes From the Storyteller—A Story for Paula*** _____

Paula is a teacher in the Juneau Teen Parent Home Visitor Head Start program. We visited Tony, who is 17, and her son Ryan. Ryan is 16 months old. Paula is waiting for me in her car. She isn't sure that Tony is going to be at home today, but she suggests that we wait a few minutes to see if Tony shows up. Paula has arranged with Tony for me to do an observation today. Tony shows up and Paula introduces us.

Paula smiles at Tony, greeting both Tony and Ryan warmly. After taking off her coat, Paula sits on the floor with Ryan, who is immediately interested in the large black bag she has with her. As Paula takes a stacking toy out of the bag for

Here the storyteller is Kay Greenough, and these are notes written to share with Paula, made on a home visit that she observed as Paula's CDA advisor.

Ryan, Tony says that Ryan has fluid behind his ears and has a cold. Paula hands Ryan a toy, and he sits down in front of her between her legs. She pats him on the back.

"Are you feeling a little sick today?" Paula says to him. He doesn't respond, and Paula asks Tony, "Have you checked about the ear tubes for Ryan? I was wondering if you had a chance to check it since our last visit." She is giving Tony her full attention as she takes the stacking donuts Ryan hands her.

"He's picked up people's names," says Tony. "He says 'Diane.' That's his aunt's name."

"So you think he's hearing OK, or do you think he needs to have the tubes put in?" asks Paula.

Tony says she still isn't sure because he is "so little."

"Should I take it off? Would you like to pull the top off?" Paula asks Ryan, smiling. It is too hard for Ryan to pull it off by himself. "I help?" she asks, and she and Ryan pull the top off together.

Ryan is interested in playing with some stencil puzzles, and Paula gives them to him. She smiles at him as she hands him a puzzle. She looks up and hands Tony a paper. "I want to show you the book orders from Scholastic," she says to Tony. "*Blueberries for Sal* is on sale, and it's one of my favorites." She offers another handout to Tony. "Would you like to read it to me, and then I'll read the next one?" asks Paula. Tony reads about Burton White's research on the first three years of life, and the stress of raising a toddler. Paula laughs warmly and Tony laughs with her.

Paula produces some books when she observes that Ryan is losing interest in the stencil puzzles. She plays with Ryan as she reads a simple book about a bear.

"Whoa," says Ryan.

"Whoa," says Paula. Ryan holds the book over his head. "Ryan hiding?" asks Paula, inviting Ryan to play hiding.

Tony gets a phone call from her husband, who is out of town. Ryan is interested in the telephone call, but Tony doesn't ask him if he wants to talk to Daddy. She puts down the telephone and picks up Ryan.

"Would you like to make the play dough now?" asks Paula. Paula has already talked with Tony about the plans for the day. Tony agrees, and she carries Ryan out to the kitchen. Paula helps Tony make a space to prepare the dough. She has provided all of the ingredients. Paula holds Ryan on her hip while Tony stirs the dough. Paula talks to both Tony and Ryan as the play dough cooks. She gives mother and child her undivided attention when she is talking and listening to each of them.

"Oh, look what Mama is doing," says Paula, showing Ryan the play dough. Paula helps Tony complete this process. She describes to Tony how Ryan can play with the dough. Paula plays with Ryan again on the floor while the dough cools. She puts away some of her things and Ryan helps her.

Paula is able to maintain attention with each of them. She is empathetic with Tony about Ryan's cold, and she shares some ideas that might help. She asks if Ryan will drink orange juice. "He likes orange juice," says Tony.

Paula has introduced dough, new puzzles, and parent resources on childrearing, along with play. The visit lasts an hour and a half. Paula is supportive and nonjudgmental with Tony, a teenage mother. Paula encourages Tony about the classes she is taking to prepare her for the GED (general educational diploma) high school equivalency exam. Paula is a good listener. She gently, gently follows through by asking questions on issues that came up at the last home visit.

Paula hugs Ryan when we go and tells Tony when she'll be coming again. The goodbye, like the greeting, is very warm.

The setting

I wrote this story for Paula, an Alaska Native Head Start home visitor, in my role as her CDA advisor. Juneau, with a population of 28,000, is the state capital and the largest community in southeast Alaska. Alaska Natives represent about 15% of the population. The other communities in the region, which are much smaller, typically have an ethnically mixed population, but some of them are Native villages. The towns and villages are scattered throughout a large island archipelago. There are no connecting roads, and only the larger communities are accessible by jet plane. Travel to the villages is by float planes and ferries, which visit some of the smaller villages only monthly. Field-based studies and teleconferences are necessarily well-developed modes of teaching at the University of Alaska Southeast (UAS), for which I work. The main campus of this small university is located in Juneau, with smaller programs in Sitka and Ketchikan.

The partnership

For the past 10 years, the university, in partnership with Central Council Tlingit and Haida Indian tribes of Alaska Head Start Program, has prepared Head Start staff for the Child Development Associate (CDA) credential. Tlingit and Haida administer 11 Head Start programs in the region. Some are primarily Alaska Native, but the culturally diverse programs in the larger communities serve a mix of low-income families, including Tlingit, Haida, Tsimshian, Filipino, and Anglo children. The programs are center-based preschool and home visitor with infant/toddler and preschool-age children.

UAS began its collaboration with Tlingit and Haida in 1982. Previously CDA training had been provided in fits and starts by trainers from outside the region, but no Head Start staff became credentialed until UAS got a small vocational education grant to provide on-site, field-based training for persons interested in earning the CDA credential or in improving their skills in early childhood education. As an independent contractor with the university, I provided this training, which successfully prepared six candidates to receive the first CDA credentials in Southeast Alaska Head Start and child care programs.

UAS recognized the CDA as the first step in the early childhood education career ladder, giving 14 credits upon completion of the credential. CDA credits could be applied to higher certificates and degrees in early childhood education given by the university. Head Start became the university's biggest customer for CDA credit.

In 1989 the partnership became more formal when UAS, in collaboration with Tlingit and Haida and Anchorage-based Rural Alaska Community Action program, was awarded a Department of Human Services (DHS) Commissioner's Discretionary Grant through the national Head Start Bureau to prepare CDA candidates from remote and isolated communities. Under this grant I moved from independent contracting to a salaried position, with an assistant qualified to advise as well.

The CDA is the minimum educational qualification required to meet the new Head Start legislative mandate that there be at least one teacher with a CDA or early childhood education degree in Head Start centers. Participating in CDA training is therefore not a choice for Head Start staff.

The project offered opportunities for training not available through the usual rural course offerings. It paid for CDA credentialing fees. It provided on-site, field-based training and on-site cluster training for CDA candidates and other

1. Colleges can support progress on the ECE career lattice (Bredekamp & Willer, 1992) by giving degree-applicable credit for CDA training.

2. Accepting credit for off-campus work designed collaboratively with community agencies reduces the exclusiveness that characterizes some institutions of higher education.

3. Where early childhood staff competence is based on experience rather than on formal education, it is important to create ways of basing college credit on experience.

early childhood providers in communities. It also trained credentialed CDAs to become CDA advisor/trainers in the villages where they live. It provided a newsletter and a monthly teleconference with advisors.

Twenty-seven teachers obtained the credential during the project. The project produced training and self-study materials as well, and the list of CDA advisors in southeast Alaska grew from 3 to 12.

Working in the project, we faced these questions:

• What is good training for culturally different staff who are mature and have extensive life experience?

• How does the fact that CDA is not a choice in Head Start affect the training design? How can it be open ended?

• How can we support socially and geographically isolated women to find their voices, to become autonomous decision makers, and to see themselves as problem solvers?

The people involved

One of the CDA candidates said to me once, "I don't talk good." She uttered this statement with frustrated force. She felt that she could not make others understand what she was saying or what she wanted to say. She was referring to a conflict she was

having with another staff member; there had been a misunderstanding, and the other person was angry and offended.

This woman did not learn her Native Athabascan as her first language. Instead, she learned to speak a variety of "village English" that isn't recognized by others as adequate to describe or represent her feelings and perceptions, thus is often not listened to.

Doubting one's intellectual capacity is all too common among the poor, rural people, and women; these overlapping populations—being widely seen as less valuable and less worthy—are seldom supported to develop their intellectual potential. Doubts about one's capacities are often accompanied by social isolation and a sense of voicelessness that undercuts one's potential for dialogue and connection with others. (Belenky, Bond, & Weinstock, 1991)

I have a personal interest in rural women's intellectual development, particularly in the development of Alaska Native women in rural communities. For the last 10 years, a major focus of my work as a college teacher and field-based trainer/advisor has been developing dialogues with Alaska Native teachers of young children to help them become autonomous thinkers and decision makers.

My growing-up experience is somewhat similar to Alaska Native women's in that I grew up both geographically and socially

Richard Ott

I was also aware of others who see the work of a farmer as unimportant. My parents often talked about this; they expressed anger, feeling slighted by interactions with people who had implied that farmers were not very smart. Both of my parents perceived that farming was undervalued and misunderstood by people who lived in town.

My own intellect began to flower when I moved away from home to go to college and later moved with my husband and two children to Alaska. I made friends with women who, like myself, were young mothers. I became active in volunteer organizations. In the 1970s I helped form a women's consciousness-raising group, which still meets regularly after 20 years. It was in this group that I learned it was possible to share perspectives, to have differences of opinion without losing friends, to feel my feelings, and to think. It was also in this group that I learned that the source of my problems and the solutions to them lay within myself. As women we often learn at an early age to distrust our thinking and our feelings. This process of talking and thinking with the support of others has helped me to find and hang onto my own voice.

isolated on a dry farm in southeastern Idaho. Although I did not experience the assaults of racism, I did experience lowered expectations, being a girl. I wanted to drive tractors and trucks, but I couldn't because girls in my family were not allowed to do those things. As a young woman it was clear to me that I was expected to marry; and while a woman might have a college education, women in this community rarely worked outside the home. The woman's role on the farm was extremely important: a farmer, like an ice hunter or fisherman, depends on the support of a woman in the home. The role is defined by self-sacrifice and caring for others; its tasks follow the demands of seasonal harvests, food gathering, and preserving.

Silent Knowers: People who hold this outlook doubt their capacities for learning in most if not all aspects of their lives. Having been raised in isolation with few mediated learning experiences, these women have had a difficult time developing representational thought and skills for participating in a dialogue. Because they experi-

Nila Rinehart, director of Tlingit-Haida Head Start, observes, "Women of color have to deal with bias on two levels: sexism *and* racism. This fact alone strikes the inner core of who we are. Some of us Native women become stronger because of it. Others become numbed by it."

ence difficulty learning from words and because they have so little confidence in their own ability to speak, the silent knowers think of themselves as virtually deaf and dumb. (Belenky et al., 1991)
    When people cannot represent their ideas easily, they are likely to think of words more as weapons than as a means for communicating meanings back and forth. (Belenky et al., 1991)

The most common approach to educating people accustomed to silent knowing is to give them The Word from some external source—the Word of God, the word of authorities, the word of those in power. Those people who believe the words they are given become received knowers.

Received Knowers: That one learns by listening to others is the basic assumption of received knowers. Here learning is equated with receiving, remembering, and returning the words of the others—the 3 r's. (Belenky et al., 1991)

Received knowing is functional in stable societies where elders have the answers to questions about how life is to be lived; it becomes insufficient in a changing society where new sorts of decisions must be made. No Alaska Native community is isolated economically, politically, or culturally, therefore intellectual isolation no longer serves any community well. In the face of change, both *subjective knowing*—confidence in one's own capacity to think—and *procedural knowing*, which challenges people to learn through intellectual engagement with other knowers, are essential tools for effective problem solving (Belenky, Clinchy, Goldberger, & Tarule, 1986).

Head Start challenges Alaska Natives, both adults and children, to become effectively bicultural. Teachers must be able to draw both on their cultural traditions and on national guidelines for developmentally appropriate early childhood education.

Native Alaskan Head Start teachers are people who are considered leaders in their communities. They are hired because both national Head Start and local grantees place a high priority on hiring people knowledgeable about the local community and its children and families. Often they have been Head Start parents and have experience both with children and with the agency. Although they may not have the skills defined by national standards in early childhood education, they are mature, responsible community members in whom the community has confidence. To treat them as people who do not know is insulting. To challenge them to reflect on their teaching respects their experience and their competence.

This is the challenge we face as CDA advisors to Head Start staff. Providers of training often define their job as showing the trainee what needs to be done. When training is conducted as telling and showing, it is assumed that trainees will receive, remember, and return the words and be able to demonstrate the told behaviors after receiving. One of the first lessons I learned was that telling and showing teachers what to do did not develop autonomy, nor did it foster the capacities for self-observation and self-

1. To "find one's voice" is a significant step in recognizing oneself as competent.

2. Many early childhood educators are women who—for reasons of social class, race, language, and culture, as well as gender—have been denied a voice.

3. Inviting speech, listening attentively, and entering into dialogue is the process by which a facilitator can enable people who have been voiceless to begin taking their power.

4. In any time and place characterized by rapid social change, the power to speak up is crucial for teachers, parents, and children.

reflection needed by a teacher in an isolated early childhood program.

Staff development strategies

In my work as CDA advisor, the strategies I have used to support teachers' self-reflection include observations of their classrooms and home visits, selective intervention with children to model problem solving, dialogue on the observations, and note taking to support the teacher's writing of her CDA portfolio. Our project has also developed self-study materials useful for sustaining the advising process at a distance.

Observations

The CDA credentialing program asks candidates to describe what they do, why they do it, and how it shows they are competent teachers of young children. Most of the teachers I work with have difficulty describing this process in their own words, especially in writing. My assistant, Linda Squibb, and I begin the process of developing dialogue with teachers by making informal observations of children and teachers to be used as subject matter for the dialogue.

To build nonauthoritarian relationships with CDA candidates, we begin our visits by focusing our observations on children. We describe children's behavior and annotate our descriptions, naming what we see in terms of the theory we are teaching. I use the CDA functional areas for this purpose, writing in the margin of the observation the competencies that the situation or the behavior indicates are present. In this way I try to make clear why I'm excited about what I've observed and why I think it's important. Here is an example.

Six boys are playing with dinosaurs in the block area.

"I want one of the long necks," says Dylan (there are several kinds of dinosaurs, and some of them have long necks).—SOCIAL

"Mind your own business," says Gary.—SOCIAL

Dylan grabs one of the "long necks" and runs over to the sand table, which has cornmeal in it. All of the cornmeal has been scooped up into a large metal mixing bowl. He buries the "long neck" in the bowl, looking back at Gary and the others. He takes the "long neck" out again. He goes back to the group and picks up a stegosaurus that is lying on the floor by the other boys. He is ignored by the boys. Dylan leaves the long neck with David and takes the stegosaurus. Nobody seems to mind this, and David picks up the "long neck."

When I share an observation with a teacher, I ask her what her role has been in the situation and how she sees it. She adds or changes details in the observation for accuracy. The observation is of children, but in a detailed observation the program and the teacher's role are evident. All of the teachers comment that they are amazed that they do so many of the CDA indicators. They say things like "I didn't realize Program Management is . . . " or "It is really helpful to have you write the CDA functional areas in the observation because I didn't think I was doing all those things."

Most learning experience that received knowers have is with experts (elders, teachers, trainers), rules, standards, and authorities (Belenky et al., 1991). The CDA materials, Head Start Performance Standards, and NAEYC's developmentally appropriate practice guidelines are all national standards for teacher behavior and practice. Other than naming the CDA functional areas, I stay away from trying to connect teachers' behavior with these standards; my goal is for teachers to make their own connections when they are ready.

We move on to observations of teachers, which we write up as narrative descriptions of what the teacher did with the children. Stories that accurately represent for teachers are not glowing accolades, but we do choose to focus on strengths. One teacher shared Linda's story about her with her supervisor as part of her evaluation process.

When I have written a story (like that for Paula, with which this chapter begins), I give it to the candidate before we talk. I ask her to underline the points that are important for her (a technique I learned from Marjorie Fields, University of Alaska Southeast). Underlining seems to help candidates identify the significant words in the story in the process of naming and making meaning for themselves.

In the early days of CDA training, formal observations for the purpose of documenting competence were done on the advisor's first or second visit to the community, as time and money for visits were limited. Candidates saw these observations as evaluations, which did not facilitate trust building. I became acutely aware of how dreaded formal CDA observations were when I saw the discomfort on candidates' faces.

CDA's new observation instrument is also threatening for candidates because the observer often isn't able to see evidence for a particular indicator, so that check mark area is left blank. As Linda said to me, "They think they aren't doing a good job because every blank isn't checked," an understandable reaction by Native people with many experiences of failure in educational systems. Because we have learned that informal observations are more effective in facilitating dialogue, we now leave the formal observation process until the end of the training, when the candidate has more trust in us

---

1. Beginning classroom observations with a focus on the *teacher's* behavior can be threatening, raising fears of being evaluated.

2. Beginning classroom observations with notes on *children's* behavior focuses both the observer's and the teacher's attention where it should be—on what is happening for children.

3. In dialogue on the observations, the teacher's behavior in the situation comes up naturally for shared reflection.

---

and more understanding of herself and her capabilities.

Informal observations establish non-authoritarian relationships with CDA candidates. They are a form of practice in which candidates become familiar with the presence of an observer in the classroom.

Intervention to model problem solving

At times, when I am observing, a teacher involved in activity needs help in changing her behavior to provide for children's needs. Intervention is a risky but potentially useful response. If I have a good sense that the teacher trusts me and that the time is right, I may model for a teacher or suggest alternative behavior by playing with the children. I take this risk only when I believe I have enough trust built with the teacher that I won't be undermining her by my action. Sometimes a moment like this one presents itself.

Kathy was playing with children who were sliding some new plastic dinosaurs down a ramp she had set up on the block shelf. The sliders were having fun, but the rest of the children were running around snatching dinosaurs when they could get them. Other children were aimless, not engaged in constructive play of any kind. Kathy was completely involved in supervising the sliders and fending off the dinosaur stealers.

I was observing this pandemonium. I laid down my notebook, moved to sit on the floor next to the ramp, and asked, "Would anyone like to play blocks and make some corrals for the dinosaurs?" I found myself immediately engaged in facilitating block play with four children who had been watching or stealing.

Kathy looked relieved. "Do you think I should just play with them like this?" she asked. "I am always so worried that I will interfere with their play." We played in the blocks with the children for a long time,

and as we did we were able to have little snatches of conversation about what was "interfering" and what was "facilitating."

Later when Kathy and I were alone together, sharing the observation, I asked her how she would distinguish interfering from helping children learn to play. She said she thought that children should "know how to play." I asked her how she used to play. She described all of the outdoor games she played as a child, but then she realized that she was remembering her play as a child older than those she teaches. She remarked that she'd learned how to play from the older children. We had a terrific conversation, and she realized that it was okay for her to play; her biggest problem was that the children really didn't know how to play very well.

Kathy has continued to play and writes that she likes what is happening to her. "I am more relaxed. I don't try to control things so." She commented in her portfolio draft that she "let go" when children were doing a painting activity and "went with the flow."

Dialogue on the observation

Talking about the observations is another important part of the process of finding a voice. I find that it is difficult for the teachers with whom I work to conceptualize their intellectual strengths. They often feel at a loss for words when they are expected to talk about what they know. The observation is concrete evidence of what they do. When we talk about observations, teachers always add comments. I am amazed at how accurately teachers remember what happened. If I miss a comment or action in the observation, teachers always seem to have the missing words or behaviors to fill in the blanks. We both are actively sharing, reflecting, and correcting the account of what happened.

During this discussion I often ask questions to which I don't know the answers—

a criterion that helps me avoid loaded questions that are really criticisms. I have been challenged to watch my tone of voice, body language, and rapidity of speech as well. It is difficult, I have repeatedly found, for a fast-moving Anglo-American to adopt a slower pace, to take time to listen and reflect back what is said, and to select patterns of speech congruent with those of my partner in the dialogue.

The dialogue on the observation provides many opportunities for the teacher to share her perspective and to hear mine. As I name the teacher's behaviors for her, my objective is that she will become able to name her behavior for herself. I am careful to build self-esteem by focusing on the "growing edge"—that is, on the strengths that I observe in children and in the program. Teachers often ask for more information after going through an observation. I make suggestions about filmed and written materials and then provide them if the teacher expresses interest.

Writing for the CDA portfolio

When teachers and I discuss the observations, we also talk about the process of writing about observations in order to demonstrate competence in the 13 functional areas. Part of the process is my role as scribe because during the dialogue I write down the ideas the teacher expresses. I give these ideas and comments to the teacher as concrete evidence of how she has represented her ideas in words written down.

An autobiography is also part of the CDA portfolio. The autobiography is a way for the candidate to represent herself and her past, and it is a pattern of how she learns. It is also a pattern of how she has taught herself to be a good teacher. Many CDA candidates need help in naming the pattern, however; their first-draft stories are very brief and reveal little about themselves.

When I read a biography that tells me little, I invite the candidate to talk about it and I ask questions. With permission, I write down the candidate's additional comments and ideas, which I give to her when we finish talking. As with the observations, candidates always have more to say about themselves when they are supported and given permission to talk about their lives. One candidate said that she felt embarrassed talking so much about herself; she had been taught that it wasn't a good idea to "toot your own horn." But when she

---

1. Teachers are competent "rememberers" of events in their classrooms. Shared observations help them to reconstruct events in detail.

2. Asking *genuine questions*—those about which the questioner is curious and to which only the teacher has the answer—is an honest and empowering approach to increasing teachers' skills in observation, reflection, and dialogue.

3. Focus on program *strengths* affirms teachers' competence while leaving room for them to raise their own genuine questions about how to make things even better.

4. Building bridges from teachers' strengths toward the skills they need to develop—for example, writing down their oral language as notes for their own writing—is a facilitative approach to supporting growth in competence.

read the notes I had made, she said, "It showed me that I really have done a lot. I didn't realize I had done so much."

The biographies also give my assistant, Linda, and me ideas for resource materials that will have personal meaning to candidates. We invite the candidates to explore materials that represent the actions, beliefs, and values they have represented in their autobiographies.

Self-study materials

During the project we also developed a series of self-study materials. Their design reflected our past experiences in Head Start training, in which we had found that teachers made changes in their teaching and in their personal lives when they were able to get in touch with their own childhood experiences and relate those experiences to their present lives (Jones, 1984, 1986).

The self-study materials ask the candidate to remember and reflect on how she was treated, taught, and talked to as a child in each of the 13 functional areas. She is also asked to observe children. Teachers thus have a way to reflect and then dialogue with us, in writing and when we are on site, about the relationships they see in their behavior with the children they teach and what they would like to change. One teacher wanted me to know that "the self-study materials changed my life." She was making connections for herself through the process of reflecting on how she had been socialized and taught.

Our staff-development strategies run counter to the view that teachers with limited skills need to be shown and told what to do. Instead, we use observation, dialogue, self-reflection, provisioning (sharing resource materials), caring, and supporting as our strategies for providing culturally sensitive training. This process takes longer than telling or showing. The model looks like this:

Coming out of silence: Teachers find their voices

Alaska Natives are used to being excluded and silenced. The history of Alaska Native education is a history of replacing the Native languages with English and replacing Native ways of learning with non-Native formal schooling. Some Alaska Native women and men are reluctant to speak about what they know until they get to know and trust an outsider and become confident that the outsider will take the time to listen respectfully. Out of many experiences of not being heard, silence becomes, for some persons, the only powerful defense.

Received knowers do not imagine that their own experience and ideas can be a source of knowledge; they are dependent on the standards, directions and authority of others. The ability to listen and to gain meaning from the world of others is of the utmost importance. It makes possible the entrance into the shared culture of one's community. However, while received knowers possess these abilities and put great faith in language for transmitting knowledge, their understanding of symbols and interpretive powers of mind are quite limited. They are not yet aware of the mind's capacity for interpreting reality. They think of themselves as passive receptacles who learn automatically by hearing and memorizing materials without mental modifications of any sort. They confuse the name with the referent. They have not realized that words and other mental representations can only approximate events, or that a single event can be represented quite differently from varied perspectives. Lacking these understandings, received knowers assume that any problem has only one right answer—that something is either right or wrong. (Belenky et al., 1991)

Some Alaska Native Head Start teachers have learned to distrust the information and stories that outside trainers and consultants have brought to the training situation. As one teacher pointed out, "Every time we go to one of the trainings they tell us something different" (urban teachers have been heard to say the same thing; see Chapter 4). On-site observations revealed that teachers were not implementing the information they had received, particularly if the information was open ended rather than clear about the "right way." I once had a teacher ask me, "Why don't you teach us?" as we concluded a session in which I was asking them what they thought about my shared observations. When I asked what they would like me to do, she said, "I want you to teach us some activities to do with the kids." Observations also revealed that teachers were asking children closed questions that require right answers, and children were often silent and nonresponsive.

While teachers were often surveyed to identify problems to be addressed in training sessions, they were given little opportunity to wrestle with the problems as a group, to dialogue with each other, and to problem-solve together. Where breakdown of traditional community and family decision-making structures had occurred without being replaced by structures enabling teachers to evolve their own ideas and solutions to problems, teachers tended to keep returning to old, ineffective ways of working with children.

I was convinced that most training isn't useful unless it's designed so that people have to struggle with their own problems. I also believed that not giving teachers choices among in-service opportunities had a lot to do with their not implementing what they were taught in training sessions. Because a degree in early childhood education or a CDA credential is now required at every site by national Head Start guidelines, whether or not to work on the CDA is not, officially, a choice for teachers. I observed, however, that some staff members manage to exercise choice by procrastinating, waiting for someone else—usually the supervising teacher—to complete the credential. I wanted staff to have some authorized choices, as well.

Tlingit and Haida agency administrators were looking for more effective approaches to staff development. They agreed that attendance at group in-service trainings in Juneau should be made a choice and, further, that sessions should be planned as facilitated problem solving rather than as presentations by outside experts. So, well in advance, we sent Head Start staff a detailed agenda of planned activities to help them decide whether or not they wanted to attend. Because only those who wanted to participate came, and because the agenda was built around storytelling by the par-

Richard Ott

ticipants about themselves and the events and problems at their sites, the outcomes included increased morale, team building and joint problem solving, and more effective communications among staff.

As in-service coordinator I acted as facilitator initially; later some community people filled this role. We spent the first half-day on introductions in large and small groups, using play and imagery as well as words. ("Tell us something about yourself. With a partner, do body drawings of each other. Decorate your drawing to show who you are in the lives of children in your program. Tell us what your decorations mean.") [The detailed agenda for this three-day in-service is available from the author.] In the role of "floater," I moved among groups to help if they got stuck; I maintained responsibility for the structure and for timekeeping, but plans were flexible and timing was relaxed. We moved into problem solving with an activity that included talking in pairs, writing (as dialogue with self), and talking in the large group, using these starting points:

• What do you remember about your parents' ways of solving problems? How did they do it?

• List three problems that you find easy to solve (the problems can be those that arise at home, at work, or with family or friends; they don't have to be problems associated with teaching).

• Complete these sentences:
  —Finding solutions to problems is hard because...
  —The cause of my problem is...
  —A solution to my problem is...

A variety of problem-solving activities followed, with group brainstorming used to help generate solutions. These in-services have been rated by staff as highly meaningful; one outcome is that many who participated in them are now involved in personal counseling and healing work.

All in-service training could be applied toward CDA credit by credential candidates. Staff who chose not to attend had other training options, including on-site CDA advising and problem solving as well as use of the self-study materials described earlier. Our partnership has continued to explore ways of providing choices in staff development, even within the requirement of a CDA. Through making, implementing, and discussing their choices, we have found, teachers find themselves with increasingly effective voices.

What was taught, what was learned, and what are the implications?

Here are basic principles our partnership uses in its approach to CDA advising:

1. Work with teachers should start on the framework of strengths and competencies the teacher already has.

2. Staff development experiences will foster self-reflection and self-observation if teachers have opportunities to identify— and support to solve—their own problems.

3. Teachers will develop the capacity to self-observe and self-reflect when observations of children and teachers are modeled and shared within a nonauthoritarian, nonevaluative, respectful relationship.

4. An advisor can help teachers name and analyze their experience by writing and discussing both detailed behavioral descriptions and names for those behaviors that connect them with national standards for practice in early childhood education. Such shared dialogue will cultivate the teacher's capacity to make changes in her behavior with children and to provide a rich learning environment for children.

5. Teachers accustomed to received knowing will experience the possibility of more complex levels of learning and thinking only if they are given significant choices, in order to practice generating ideas that can lead to choosing their own actions.

Showing and telling someone what to do may be useful for a time, but unless a teacher can think for herself, her training will break down when new problems arise that she has never dealt with. Rural, isolated teachers need to be able to figure things out, decide what they need, and know how to get it. To become an autonomous thinker, a teacher must have the capacity to observe, reflect, and provide a rich learning environment for children. To model this process we observe children and teachers, and we spend time reflecting with teachers when we share our observations. We provide materials for teachers based on what they tell us, offering connections to new resources. This process shows teachers the continuity and value of their experience. We know we are succeeding when we see teachers doing with children what we are doing with them; although at a different level, the process is the same. They are observing children, creating the learning environment, and reflecting with them on what they are doing, in order to develop higher levels of thinking and the capacity for autonomous problem solving.

For further information

Greenough, K. (1987). *The changer and the changed: Teaching and consulting in rural southeast Alaska.* Unpublished master's thesis, Pacific Oaks College, Pasadena, CA.

Greenough, K. (1990). *Head Start in Hoonah, Alaska* (videotape and study questions). Juneau, AK: University of Alaska.

Greenough, K. (1990). *Learning about myself* (self-study materials). Juneau, AK: University of Alaska.

Other suggested readings

Ayers, W. (1989). *The good preschool teacher: Six teachers reflect on their lives.* New York: Teachers College Press.

Coles, R. (1977). *Children of Crisis. Vol. 4: Eskimos, Chicanos, Indians.* Boston: Little Brown.

Cronin, S. (1991). *On preparing bilingual early childhood professionals.* Occasional paper. Pasadena, CA: Pacific Oaks College.

Gonzales-Mena, J. (1993). *Multicultural issues in child care.* Mountain View, CA: Mayfield.

Greenbaum, W. (1974). America in search of a new ideal: An essay on the rise of pluralism. *Harvard Educational Review, 44*(3), 411–440.

Greenberg, P. (1969). *The devil has slippery shoes: A biased biography of the Child Development Group of Mississippi.* New York: Macmillan. (Reissued for Head Start's 25th anniversary by Youth Policy Institute, P.O. Box 40132, Washington, DC)

Heilbrun, C.G. (1988). *Writing a woman's life.* New York: Ballantine.

Jones, E. (1988). *Reflection and dialogue: Ways to grow staff.* Keynote, First National Institute for Head Start Education Coordinators, Washington, DC. Occasional paper. Pasadena, CA: Pacific Oaks College.

Kleinfeld, J. (1972). *Effective and ineffective teachers of Native high school students.* Fairbanks: University of Alaska, Institute of Social and Economic Research.

Paley, V. (1979). *White teacher.* Cambridge, MA: Harvard University Press.

Witherell, C., & Noddings, N. (Eds.). (1991). *Stories lives tell: Narrative and dialogue in education.* New York: Teachers College Press.

References

Belenky, M.F., Bond, L.A., & Weinstock, J.S. (1991). *From silence to voice: Developing the ways of knowing.* Unpublished manuscript, University of Vermont, Burlington, VT.

Belenky, M.F., Clinchy, B.M., Goldberger, N.R., & Tarule, J.M. (1986). *Women's ways of knowing: The development of self, voice and mind.* New York: Basic Books.

Bredekamp, S., & Willer, B. (1992). Of ladders and lattices, cores and cones: Conceptualizing an early childhood professional development system. *Young Children, 47*(3), 47–50.

Jones, E. (1984). Training individuals: In the classroom and out. In J. Greenman & R. Fuqua (Eds.), *Making day care better: Training, evaluation, and the process of change* (pp. 185–201). New York: Teachers College Press.

Jones, E. (1986). *Teaching adults: An active learning approach.* Washington, DC: NAEYC.

To contact the author, write Kathrin Greenough, Early Childhood Education, School of Education and Liberal Arts, University of Alaska Southeast, 11120 Glacier Highway, Juneau, AK 99803.

I n the Seattle metropolitan area, vocational instructors made
weekly visits to a wide variety of child care centers, where they
were expected to contribute to the improvement of program quality.
It was up to these instructors to figure out how, and they had autonomy in doing so. Staff were generally not voluntary participants,
nor were they necessarily experienced, competent, or planning to
remain in the field. In contrast to the experienced, stable staffs with
which David Beers and Kay Greenough worked in Native American
Head Start, Margie Carter encountered constant staff turnover in this
urban setting.

Under such conditions, can a trainer become a facilitator and storyteller? In this chapter Margie describes how and why she did. The
changes she made in her approach over a number of years grew out of
her frustrations and continuing curiosity: How can child care workers
really understand developmentally appropriate practice? Can I help
them construct knowledge for themselves through collaborative observation and reflection?

Chapter 3

Catching Teachers "Being Good": Using Observation To Communicate

Margie Carter

_____ **Notes From the Storyteller*** _____

Entering Terry's classroom, I sat down to begin my weekly observation. I used the form I had recently invented, with room for both notes and comments to be discussed with Terry during naptime (in the notes, T is for Terry).

Focus: Active learning opportunities	Date: 10/7/88
Observations	**Comments**
At 9:00 A.M. the children came from outside, hung up coats and, without adult reminders, came to sit for circle time. Terry immediately sat on the floor with those who arrived first, while aides helped others with coats.	Great that kids who were ready didn't have to wait.

_____

* Here the storyteller is Margie Carter, and this is an observation-with-comments she made, as a child care trainer, for discussion with Terry, the teacher.

Observations	Comments
T: "Do you know a song we can sing while we're waiting?" Someone suggested the alphabet song, which they immediately began singing. There were a few songs with motions, roll call, and a dismissal into small groups.	You allowed them to choose a song. Got them actively involved so that even those who don't sing have an option of motions to do.
(9:12 A.M.) T: "I need some help pulling out the table for my group." The children quickly moved to help and then settled into seats. T held up a can of shaving cream and asked if they knew what it was. She then went from child to child, putting shaving cream on the table in front of them in the shape of a letter to guess. They were told to "go ahead and play in it." T sat down with some in front of her, played and drew in her cream, talking with kids as she did. They talked about how the cream felt, what they were making, and things going on at home. As the children said they were done and wanted to wash up, T let them go to the bathroom, one at a time.	Smooth transition. Again, no waiting. Immediate involvement and active participation.

Wonderful opportunity for sensory exploration of their own choice. A range of topics emerging as they played. Did you hear any that you might want to follow up on later? |
| (9:28 A.M.) T goes to wash her hands and returns with paper towels and a sponge, starting to clean up the table. | Would some dishpans of water and towels on a nearby table have worked to use for washing up? It might have made supervision of cleanup easier and possibly led to some further water activities. |
| Immediately several kids said they wanted to clean up. Nathan pointed to T's sponge, saying "I want that." "What *is* that?" T asked. "A sponge." T gave it to him. | I wasn't sure why you asked this. Do you have more sponges that could be used? |

Observations	Comments
Nathan moved the sponge back and forth on the table and said, "I'm washing my car window. Look. I'm at the gas station washing my car window." T didn't respond. She may not have heard.	If you had heard this comment, how could you have extended the activity?
When most of the table was clean, T started individual kids on planning with pens and a clean-wipe board. She let them draw, then asked "What did you make?" "Blocks," Jenny answered. "What are you going to do with blocks?"	
As the board seemed difficult to erase, T suggested replacing it with a tray of salt in which they could use their finger to sketch. "Tell me about it." "Puzzles," said Taiko. "What area are the puzzles in?" "Table Toy Area."	A good indication of your awareness of potential frustration. Substitution allowed for the representation to continue without disruption.
As children were off to activities, one child returned to the table and asked to play with the clean-wipe board. T explained that it wasn't erasing well but could still be used if he wanted.	Another good example of allowing child to pursue interests.
(9:55 A.M.) Nicky asked to use the new tape recorder. T sent him to the office to get batteries. A small group gathered around to see the new player. T opened the package and silently began to figure out how to insert batteries and microphone jacks.	This is an occasion for further active exploration and language. How could the children have been involved in figuring things out with you? Things you could have said? Questions that might have promoted thinking and exploration?
	Are you interested in doing further activities based on this experience with batteries?

Terry responded positively to the comments I had written and thought that my suggestion of having dishpans of water, towels, and sponges was a good way to enable the children to continue in self-help without checking with her or having to leave the room to clean up.

Most of our discussion was focused on the missed opportunities with the tape recorder and batteries. She acknowledged that it never occurred to her to talk out loud about what she was trying to figure out and to trust that, in fact, some of the children might be able to problem-solve how to insert the batteries. I asked if she had other battery-operated objects in the classroom or materials that she could bring from home to explore batteries and their use in a small group. She has a flashlight that the children periodically use in the room, but she couldn't think of anything else. I clarified that I was not suggesting she go out and buy battery-operated toys; rather, I thought it would be helpful to just keep in mind that putting objects together and taking them apart was very much a part of how children learn. She expressed a concern that the last tape recorder had gotten broken from misuse. I suggested that she identify the children who knew how to use the tape recorder properly and have them demonstrate to the rest of the group. I also suggested she give the children some screwdrivers and pliers to use in taking apart the broken tape recorder, making it clear why this was acceptable and that it shouldn't be done to the new one. Terry left, saying that she would keep in mind the idea of involving children in the introduction of new equipment in the room.

The setting

This observation in Terry's classroom took place early in my experience as one of 30 (fewer in some years) part-time early childhood education instructors employed by Renton Vocational-Technical Institute (RVTI; now Renton Technical College) in the Seattle area. The child and family department of RVTI had a program of child care instruction that involved instructors' making three-hour weekly visits to child care sites to offer on-the-job training. The program was funded by a combination of fees and Washington state funds for vocational education, which could be used to upgrade personnel already employed in industry—including child care.

Participation by centers was voluntary except for centers under contract with the city of Seattle to take low-income children. These centers were expected to provide staff training under the terms of their contract, and it was assumed that all teachers would participate. Other centers paid a fee of $10 per staff member per quarter, and staff were thereby registered as RVTI students receiving off-campus instruction.

RVTI always had a waiting list for the training program. To be eligible to participate, a center had to have at least five staff members working with the children at 10 A.M. Because the program as a whole had to average 11 staff members per center, larger centers had some priority. Centers could stay in the program as long as they liked.

The Seattle metropolitan area, with a population of about two million, includes a variety of urban and suburban communities. Child care is available through nonprofit agencies, churches, private for-profit groups, and public sponsorship. Child care centers in Washington must meet licensing requirements, but these do not include preservice training or educational qualifications for staff. Anyone 18 years of age or older who passes health and fingerprint checks can be employed as a full-time child care worker. Wages are low (average $5.21 per hour in 1988) (Whitebook, Phillips, & Howes, 1989), and staff turnover is 43% in any given six-month period.

State licensing requires that a program supervisor with 45 credits in early childhood education be on the premises 20 hours a week. This is usually, but not always, the director. Directors are better paid and more likely to stay in their positions, although annual turnover is still significant. Of the many demands on directors, not the least of these is the constant hiring of new staff from an ever-diminishing pool of qualified applicants. RVTI trainers have been the cornerstone of director support and access to resources for staff training.

Cast of characters

RVTI's role in this training partnership was administrative; it brought the players together. Trainers (although our official title was "part-time instructor," our supervisor and all paperwork referred to us as trainers) were provided with a list of possible training objectives and were assigned to centers. In theory the center interviewed and chose a trainer; in practice RVTI made the match. If either the center or a trainer requested a change, however, it was always granted. We were trusted to work independently with little supervision except for an annual trainers' meeting and two evaluative observations of our work. Old-timers took new trainers under their wing and taught them the ropes.

Trainers hired by RVTI were expected to have a B.A. in early childhood education, management experience, and at least five years' work in quality child care centers. We were employed for 3 to 21 hours a week, some of us working at one or two sites, some at six or seven. We acted as consultants to the center, working with the director, staff, and, in some cases, parents, to improve the quality of the program. Although we were well qualified in child care, most of us had little or no formal education in adult learning theory. We improvised as we went along.

Some of the trainers, especially those assigned to only one or two centers, worked on their own without much interaction with the other trainers. Others of us were eager to initiate dialogue about the complexities of our task, our questions, and our discoveries. Trainers at centers with Department of Human Resources (DHR) city contracts had two annual case-management meetings with DHR and RVTI supervisors, with public health nurses in attendance. At these meetings trainers expressed concern that we were regularly used for crisis management rather than working with directors in any systematic fashion to get to the root of the problems. DHR and RVTI responded by formalizing a goal-setting process between trainers and directors, using a list of training foci to choose from.

I found organizing a voluntary support group for trainers more useful than the

The city's child care subsidy program contracted with child care centers to take low-income children with fees paid by the Department of Human Resources (DHR)—now Health and Human Services.

Because the city's reimbursement rate was substantially lower than the actual child care fees, programs lost money when they enrolled these children. As an incentive (and to ensure that low-income children didn't get substandard care), a trainer and a public health nurse were provided without charge to participating centers. The city contracted with RVTI for the trainers.

case-management meetings. This eventually led to a request that I develop a class, Training of ECE Trainers, which I co-taught over a three-year period with Deb Curtis, another trainer. The class was very popular, averaging 30 to 40 participants each time it was offered.

Just as we were formalizing a four-quarter ECE trainers certificate program, though, RVTI responded to state budget cuts by gutting the entire on-site child care training program. As of January 1993, a redesigned program serving the City of Seattle contract centers is being administered by Seattle Central Community College.

Staff development strategies

When I began to work as a trainer at a center, I first met with the director. In some cases she had identified an individual classroom or teacher needing help; occasionally teachers had requested help. My preference was to begin working with those teachers who were eager to have me help. I found that positive experiences and recognizable changes in their classrooms would spark an interest on others' part to have me work with them, too. When directors wanted me to fix up teachers whom they saw as having problems, I tried to be responsive to their requests, but often I was able to strategize with them about making my work with interested teachers spill over to those who were initially less interested.

Because I was in the center under a contractual agreement with the director rather than at the request of teachers, I initially believed that my responsibility was to the directors, and I discussed staff strengths and weaknesses with them. If there was staff suspicion of me as evaluator, this was to some degree justified. In most cases, however, teachers soon saw me as a listening ear for their frustrations

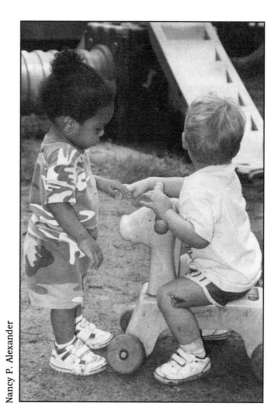

Nancy P. Alexander

and confusions and seemed pleased with my responsiveness.

I was called *trainer*, and it was evident to me that training to establish a baseline of competence was the priority in most of the classrooms I visited. At first, teachers' deficits were clearer to me than their strengths. Nevertheless I began my work in a facilitative mode with the hope of establishing trusting relationships on which teaching and learning could be built. Not wanting to intimidate staff or produce anxiety, my general approach was to present myself as a "resource person" available to answer questions and provide ideas and resources.

As people became comfortable with me, I offered direct help to improve their teaching. Through the years, in active dialogue with fellow trainers, I became more direct in my initial approach as well. I experienced a continual concern, however: If I tell people how to do it, they may do it. But they won't really understand it unless they've constructed their knowledge for themselves. It was out of this concern that my training strategies gradually moved beyond expert "telling" to facilitative "storytelling" and "broadcasting."

My strategies changed from year to year as I became familiar with the issues and thought in depth about the theoretical and practical implications of my work. As I kept trying to get teachers to reflect on their practice, I was continually reflecting on my own. Some of the teachers changed; so did I. This account of strategies is thus chronological, describing where I began, the disequilibrium I experienced, and how and why I continued to make changes.

First year

When I began making weekly visits, I was particularly conscious of the need to take time to build trust between staff members and myself. I strove to find ways to identify and work from their strengths. For most of the teachers, this was the first time an outside specialist had been available to them, and many were nervous about being judged or evaluated. I was, in fact, internally evaluating them, although for the first few months at a center I kept all of my comments positive and tried to push out of my mind's eye the things I would have liked them to be doing differently. I sat with the children at circle times, reinforcing good group behavior even when I internally questioned the length or legitimacy of that time. I helped with what I believed to be questionable art activities, lunch routines, or time-outs. My first priority was building trust.

Some of my training colleagues expressed guilt if all they did was hang around and talk. I had my own share of anxieties, but I could see the value of this low-key approach, so I ruled out guilt.

Informally moving around the classrooms, I attempted to model appropriate interactions with the children and between adults. To show respect I never interceded in a teacher's activity, but I made it clear that I was available should the teachers need a hand. I helped with housekeeping chores, playground supervision, diapering, and naptime, wanting to demonstrate that I could be useful and was willing to dirty my hands. Sometimes I brought a story or song or materials to share with the children and offered these activities as options to the teacher when I arrived. Teacher almost always were grateful, and increasingly this became part of my training. I left the material with them to use for the week, often with a related article to read. Rarely was there any interest shown in follow-up activities or discussion, and I often didn't pursue the idea myself.

During conferences with the director I attempted to "plant seeds" by raising questions, in the most innocuous way I knew how, about certain policies and practices: "Do you have any rules in the center about how time-out should be used?" "I've noticed that the children in the Bluebird Room are having trouble sitting during group time. Have you and the teachers talked about that?" "All of the teachers seem to be frazzled and using loud voices at lunchtime. Is that something you would like me to focus some training on, and if so, which room would you like me to start with?"

My goal in these conversations with directors was twofold: to alert them to an observation without sounding critical or making them defensive and to get them to authorize or legitimize my role in suggesting some changes. My relationships with all of the directors grew to the point where they began to seek my advice and call upon me for specific help. By the second half of the year, directors began to arrange for me to have meetings with the staff at least once a month. This felt like progress because there had been no staff training meetings in the past. It signaled to me that the director was valuing what I had to offer.

My role was defined as training, and that's what I assumed I should be doing. There were many obvious deficits in most programs; I felt responsible for trying to fix some of them, but I didn't feel particularly successful. Trying one strategy after another, I perceived that my training was jumping around rather than consistently moving with a clear focus.

Second and third years

Increasingly rapid staff turnover contributed to my sense of inconsistency. By the end of my second year as a trainer, half of the people I had started with had left their centers. I was continually starting over with building relationships, establishing trust, and generating some interest in training. I saw classroom after classroom get rearranged and routines and schedules reorganized. New teachers coming in wanted to make the classrooms theirs, and often they made changes with a "new look" in mind rather than with some principles about learning environ-

ments for children. There were always new faces, new rules, new routines, and new room arrangements for children to get used to. The constant changes were beginning to show in children's behaviors; they seemed less and less involved in any sustained play. An increasing number of children were being referred to as "behavior problems."

During my third year as a trainer, the "environment as curriculum" became central to my thinking. If I could get teachers to set up an interesting environment with many choices and materials available, would that provide enough stability to engross the children in play? Increasingly I felt the need for a structured approach to working with an untrained workforce in child care centers. Building trust and gradually sorting out my role in each center no longer seemed possible because new staff were coming and leaving all the time.

Fourth year

In my fourth year as trainer, I introduced a more direct approach, with observation/feedback sessions as a general strategy. I began by asking teachers to identify something in their classroom or teaching

Facilitative strategies may include the following:

1. focusing on those teachers who are most interested (and relying on spill-over to others)

2. answering questions and providing ideas and resources

3. keeping comments positive

4. helping and modeling in classrooms

5. observing teachers, with follow-up discussion

6. observing *children*, rather than teachers, to focus attention where it belongs in an early childhood classroom about which they would like some feedback. Then I developed an informal observation form to highlight what I hoped to see; and in an effort to reduce anxiety and get the teacher focused on appropriate behaviors, I gave her the option of using the form to observe me first. Following my observation we conferenced during naptime. I then observed for two more weeks, varying the structure each time. At each stage I wanted to set the teacher up by making it clear what she should be striving for and what I would be looking for.

I gave teachers the choice of whether to participate in this process and to determine what the focus should be, but the idea was mine and made most of them anxious. I don't think they complied to please me, however, rather because they knew it would give them a straight look at

Michaelyn Straub

themselves. The motivation to see oneself as others do is a clear indicator of a desire to learn and change behavior. (Terry's story at the beginning of the chapter is an example of this observation/feedback process. It worked well for her. At the end of the year, however, she left child care for a cosmetology program, hoping for a more glamorous paycheck.)

Fifth year

In response to the several strategies I had used up to this point, I saw positive changes in many classrooms. Learning environments and interactions with children had improved. Classrooms were running more smoothly, which pleased teachers and directors alike. I was still troubled, however, by the extent to which children's play was unnoticed or unappreciated and therefore continually interrupted. Although in most classrooms a time block was devoted to "free play," adults were missing its significance. They spent their time in housekeeping or recordkeeping chores, only noticing when problems arose. Or they moved about the room asking a stream of closed-ended questions: What are you making? What color is that? How many blocks are in your tower? Or they could be found continually reminding children to share, to clean up, or to put their name on their work.

During the summer I took a graduate class on observation of children with Elizabeth Prescott. In the class, working in small groups to identify a question we wanted answered through our observations, we spent mornings observing and afternoons discussing and interpreting what we had seen. Several things happened to me during this experience. I became a more skilled observer and formulator of exploratory questions; and, with no responsibilities other than to observe, I learned to focus more keenly on

> ## Facilitating Observation of Children's Play
>
> The first role of a teacher is that of observer of children. A facilitator can help teachers to
>
> **1.** observe children's *play* rather than observe to assess;
>
> **2.** observe to feed back to the children some form of representation of their play; and
>
> **3.** become increasingly skilled in observation.
>
> A facilitator can help teachers by modeling the role of observer:
>
> **1.** observing children's play and inviting teachers to observe too;
>
> **2.** talking with teachers about the play as it's happening; and
>
> **3.** documenting and "broadcasting" observations of children's play, on bulletin boards and video.
>
> As teachers get more intrigued with children's play, they become more intentional and appropriate in their actions in the classroom.

children's play and its significance. It felt like falling in love.

My previous work with teachers on observation had focused on cognitive learning objectives, leading most teachers to approach observation as an assessment tool. I began to see the limitations of this approach as a primary motivator for observing children—it tended to create myopic vision.

In some of the classrooms in which I worked, teachers were using the High/ Scope Plan/Do/Review process, in which, during review time, teachers help children recall what they did during their play. The most effective review strategy I had seen was when a teacher reviewed for the children what she had seen them doing, rather than asking the children to tell for themselves. What I liked best was the fact that this task created a new role for the teacher during play time. Her job was no longer to tell, question, or police, but rather to observe in order to be able to

feed back to the children some form of representation of their play—in story, song, pictures, or written words.

When I challenged teachers to try this new role, those with limited observation skills found it difficult; but it was a challenge they eagerly embraced. What they saw excited, pleased, and raised new questions for them. They wanted more time and skills to observe. Our discussions moved to a whole new level. It became clear to me that, as effective as my work with observation/feedback had been, I needed to shift my focus from observing teachers to thinking out loud with them about observations of the children's play. It now seemed obvious that if I didn't want the teachers to be the primary focus in the classroom, my modeling should not be making them central in my classroom observations. I should observe children and invite the teachers to observe children too.

Sixth year: Observing children, not teachers

Around this time I taught a community college class on developmentally appropriate curriculum with Deb Curtis, and I convinced some of the teachers with whom I had been working to enroll. I wanted them to have experiences to develop their understanding of the role of play in their own and children's learning. Key concepts of the course were seeing the curriculum as "loose parts" in the environment; roles for the adults other than "teaching"; and observing and planning from children's play.

The class was built around playful experiences for the adults and video clips of children delighting in play. It brought teachers together in a group for discussion, play, and mutual support, and the result was tremendous enthusiasm for a play-centered curriculum. Still, some teachers worried about learning objectives and their own ability to justify letting the children "just play all day." Would they sustain an orientation toward a play curriculum once our class ended? It seemed to me that high involvement in observing children's play would enable teachers to continue reflecting on the children's play and its significance. I concluded that the first role for teachers is that of observer.

The following year I started my on-site work with a dramatic shift: I took my focus entirely off the teachers and, instead, I thought out loud with them about my observations of the children's play. This focus is consistent with the idea that in a good early childhood classroom, most of the attention should be child centered rather than teacher directed. I began to model an interest in children's play and initiate enthusiastic discussion of "master players" (Jones & Reynolds, 1992). Standing on the sidelines, I'd talk with a teacher about the play I was observing.

I discovered that as teachers got more intrigued with children's play, they became more intentional and appropriate in their actions in the classroom. As they began to initiate conversations with me about children or activities, I gave teachers a short form to use as a way of learning observation skills. Or we'd use it together while viewing video footage I had taped in their classrooms.

Probably the most successful strategy I used to get teachers excited about children's play was to document and broadcast my observations of children at play. Moving into the role of storyteller, I made sketches or took snapshots and annotated them for "Master Players" bulletin board displays. Eventually some of the teachers began doing this them-

---

Because RVTI had a video camera available (old and funky, but functioning), I had made use of it from the beginning. At first I taped teachers' behavior for feedback; later I shifted to taping children's behavior.

My use of videotaping varied depending on teachers' response. Some teachers continually shied away from taping; others found it invaluable. In one center tapes were for teachers' private viewing at home; I filmed but never previewed or discussed the tapes with them. One center wrote a grant and got their own camera; teachers set it up on a tripod and taped themselves, then privately critiqued themselves with guidelines I had provided.

selves. The photo to the right is an example from Juanita's classroom.

Juanita had been a challenge for me. Early in our relationship I wrote,

> Juanita has a reputation for being a terrific teacher. Every inch of her room breathes creativity and attention. Based on the theme of the month, there are decorations from the entryway to the farthest corner. Most are made by her talented hand, some by the three-year-old children under her close eye. She works alone in the room with nine children. Occasionally she's dressed in a costume related to the theme.
>
> Juanita gets mixed reviews from the other eight regular staff members. Some find her a fantastic model. Others say they would never want to be like her. There is a mixture of awe, jealousy, and resentment.
>
> Once I spent time in her room, I began to unravel what troubled me most. She spent hours setting up a remarkably inviting environment and allowed very little time for the children to actually explore or experience it. Her activities and schedule were so planned out that the children never really got to their own sustained play. How could I begin to raise questions about the suitability of Juanita's classroom for three-year-old learning? The director and every parent at the center thinks Juanita is what preschool paradise is all about.

Juanita was an experienced, creative teacher, accustomed to being appreciated. Never had I come across such an overachieving teacher in child care! She continually sought opportunities for professional development and repeatedly invited me to observe and give her feedback, expressing hurt that I paid her less attention than other teachers. Looking back, I see clearly that I somewhat avoided her because I thought she needed some fixing but didn't know how to raise my questions with her.

It wasn't until I learned to express my appreciation using the storytelling role

that Juanita and I connected. The challenge of observing master players gave her a reason to stand back and see what the children might do with the amazing environment she had created. Slowly she shed her tight schedule and excess daily routines. Children were allowed to carry her materials around the room. Some of this material began to include stuff scrounged from recycling bins, yard sales, and hardware stores.

"Loose parts! Loose parts!" she called to me one morning, waving me into her room (she was taking my college class on developmentally appropriate curriculum, and loose parts in the environment was a concept [Nicholson, 1974] we were discussing). "Look how they took my lacing boards and put one here and here and here on the table. Then they tied the laces across the top and created a bridge to crawl under. I would never have thought of that."

Three teachers at Juanita's center were taking my class, and we started a Master

Players bulletin board. Juanita was the first to fill it with sketches, photographs, and dictated and teacher-scribed stories. Because she still needed an outlet for all of her creative talents, she quickly channeled them into displays of what the children did with the materials she provided for them.

One day I heard Juanita laughing all the way down the hall. When I poked my head into her room, I didn't see her at first. More laughter led me to her in the dress-ups. "Oh, here's my teacher, Margie," she exclaimed to the children. "Perhaps she'll come to our dinner party too."

"You know, Margie," she said with delight, "I think this is the teacher as player. I think this is a wonderful job."

What was taught, what was learned, and what are the implications?

Choice and empowerment seem to be the key. It's hard to give adults choices when we see changes we want them to make in their behavior. Directors and trainers frequently ask me, "What if the teacher's choice is nowhere near the area of change I want her to focus on?" We really must trust that if we build on a learning interest a teacher expresses, this will start a change process that carries over into other areas. I see this as another example of doing with adults what we hope they will do with the children.

Teaching directors to facilitate

Teaching a class on staff training and development, Deb Curtis and I have chosen to assume that center directors can spend part of their time as facilitators rather than evaluators (see discussion of this issue in the Introduction). In search of a training strategy to motivate teachers to observe children, we asked directors to enter the classrooms at their sites with a focus on the children's behavior rather than on the teachers'. This is consistent with the idea that in a good early childhood classroom, most of the attention should be child centered rather than teacher centered. We wanted directors and trainers to model an interest in children's play and to initiate enthusiastic discussion about their observations of master players.

For two weeks we asked directors and trainers to observe for the kinds of play they hope to see in children, documenting specific examples and "broadcasting" them throughout the center. Some used the idea of a bulletin board with examples of master players observed. Others made an effort to take teachers aside and point out sustained play that was occurring among children. Within a short period many reported a new excitement emerging, with teachers starting to discuss their own observations.

With an interest in children's play and the practice of observation under way, we expanded our training strategy to alert teachers to their role in planning for master players. For the next two weeks, we asked the directors and trainers to continue observing and broadcasting in the classroom but to shift the focus to environmental factors that support play. Some made use of sketches to note room arrangements that encourage sustained play. Others documented materials in one part of the room that children incorporated into their play in a different area. As these observations were shared, teachers began to see more clearly the role of the environment in children's play and to become more intentional in their planning. They were then eager for ideas and resources on learning environments.

For the final two weeks of our class, we had trainers and directors observe for examples of teacher behaviors that encourage sustained play by children. Annotated sketches, photographs, audio tapes, and videotapes were all used as tools for broadcasting. The teachers were as thrilled as the children were to have their daily activities acknowledged and represented. And, as we know is true with children, catching the teacher "being good" was contagious, and appropriate behavior became increasingly common.

Empowering teachers beyond the classroom

Teacher empowerment has been a significant outcome of this work. I have devoted energy to it while wearing several different hats. Because the RVTI training was part time, I held other jobs simultaneously. For several years I was the training coordinator at Seattle's Child and Family Resource Center, where I organized workshops for teachers, directors, and trainers and created a lending library of dramatic-play kits. I also taught evening and weekend community college classes like the class just described. This collection of roles supported my interest in building collective support networks among child care staff.

Within each center I worked hard to create mutual support. I constantly referred

teachers to each other as resources, both in conversation and through announcements in newsletters and at workshops. I took teachers to other centers to visit. As trainers began to network, we began to connect our teachers with each other, as well. Several centers began coordinating evening trainings together.

In my third year of working for RVTI, I returned to my six training sites to find that over the summer most had had close to 50% staff turnover. Chaos was again the norm, along with many developmentally questionable practices. I became enormously discouraged. What good is all that I have learned about facilitating staff growth when program quality is continually eroded by staff turnover?

It was at this point that I helped to begin what has become a national effort to address the child care staffing and salary crisis: the Worthy Wages Campaign. In Seattle this work was begun by directors and ECE colleagues, who organized an annual parade through the downtown business area. As a follow-up to the National Child Care Staffing Study (Whitebook et al., 1989), I worked with several trainers and advocates on a teacher-empowerment retreat, which we

> When staff turnover is high,
>
> 1. continuing baseline training is needed;
>
> 2. focus on the "environment as curriculum" offers the possibility of greater stability for children; and
>
> 3. moving beyond the center into collective action on behalf of worthy wages in early childhood programs becomes essential to increase quality.

called "Finding Our Voices." Out of that the Worthy Wages Task Force was formed, and after several years of tenuous existence, it has finally stabilized with its own strong leadership. Five of the eight core leaders are from centers where I have been the trainer. Some members of this task force are emphasizing solutions through legislative and corporate support systems. My own interest is in assisting child care staff to find their own voices for self-advocacy and problem solving. Today I can hardly set foot inside a child care program without referring to work on staff salaries.

As external facilitators and broadcasters, several RVTI trainers have been instrumental in assisting many directors and teachers to find their voices within their centers—with other staff, parents, and boards—and within the metropolitan area—becoming part of such activities as a speakers' bureau, union organizing, street theater, article writing, and media interviews. Some have gone on for further education, while others have become officers in AEYC Affiliates, our citywide directors' association, and other community organizations and agencies.

We have learned—and taught—that increasing quality in child care can't happen in any lasting way within individual centers. But networks of early childhood personnel in active dialogue with each other about quality teaching *and* about the working conditions we share can hope to make a difference.

For further information

Carter, M., regular column on staff training in *Child Care Information Exchange*.

Carter, M. (1991). *Staff development in early childhood education: Training approaches*. Unpublished master's thesis, Pacific Oaks College, Pasadena, CA.

Carter, M. (Producer). (1991). *Worthy work, worthless wages* [video]. A 15-minute video chronicling the Seattle child care community's efforts to address the staffing crisis. Available for $20 from Child Care Employee Project, 6536 Telegraph Avenue, A201, Oakland, CA 94609.

Carter, M., & Curtis, D. (Directors and Producers). (1993). *Making news, making history* [video]. A 15-minute video chronicling the growing national Worthy Wage Campaign grassroots movement. Available for $30 from the National Center for the Early Childhood Work Force, 6536 Telegraph Avenue, A201, Oakland, CA 94609.

Carter, M., & Jones, E. (1990, October). The teacher as observer: The director as role model. *Child Care Information Exchange, 75*, 27–30.

Carter, M., Jones, E., & Lakin, M.B. (1991). *Ideas for staff development*. Occasional paper. Pacific Oaks College, Pasadena, CA. (includes reprints of the Carter & Jones and Jones & Carter articles)

Jones, E., & Carter, M. (1991, January/February). Teacher as scribe and broadcaster: Using observation to communicate—Part 2. *Child Care Information Exchange, 77*, 35–38.

Other suggested readings

Brooks, J.G. (1990, February). Teachers and students: Constructivists forging new connections. *Educational Leadership, 47*(5), 68–71.

Caldwell, B.M., & Hilliard, A.G. (1985). *What is quality child care?* Washington, DC: NAEYC. (Also available as videos)

Carter, M., & Curtis, D. (in press). *Training teachers: A harvest of theory and practice.* St. Paul, MN: Redleaf Press.

Child Care Employee Project. (1988). *Working for quality child care.* Oakland, CA: Author.

Child Care Employee Project. (1990). *Strategies for raising child care salaries.* Oakland, CA: Author.

Child Care Workers Alliance. (1990). *Changing your working conditions: The first step.* Minneapolis: Author.

Copple, C. (1991). *Quality matters: Improving the professional development of the early childhood work force.* Washington, DC: NAEYC.

Csikszentmihalyi, M. (1975). *Beyond boredom and anxiety: The experience of play in work and games.* Chapter 11. The politics of enjoyment (pp. 179–206). San Francisco: Jossey-Bass.

Edwards. C., Forman, G., & Gandini, L. (Eds.). (1993). *The hundred languages of children: The Reggio Emilia approach to early childhood education.* Norwood, NJ: Ablex.

Goffin, S.G., & Lombardi, J. (1988). *Speaking out: Early childhood advocacy.* Washington, DC: NAEYC.

Hilliard, A.G. (1974). Moving from abstract to functional teacher education: Pruning and planting. In B. Spodek (Ed.), *Teacher education* (pp. 7–23). Washington, DC: NAEYC.

Jones, E. (1984). Training individuals: In the classroom and out. In J. Greenman & R. Fuqua, *Making day care better: Training, evaluation and the process of change* (pp. 185–201). New York: Teachers College Press.

Morin, J. (1989). *Taking action: A proposal for improving compensation in the early childhood field through employee activism.* Madison, WI: Wisconsin AEYC.

Morin, J. (1989). Viewpoint. We can force a solution to the staffing crisis. *Young Children, 44*(6), 18–19.

Morin, J. (1991). *Taking matters into our own hands: A guide to unionizing in the child care field.* Oakland, CA: Child Care Employee Project.

Randall, M. (1991). *Walking to the edge: Essays of resistance.* Boston: South End Press.

Riley, D. (1983). Observation and story-telling: Useful tools in preschool consulting. In S. Stine (Ed.), *Administration: A bedside guide.* Pasadena, CA: Pacific Oaks College.

Shor, I. (1980). *Critical teaching and everyday life.* Boston: South End Press.

Stalmack, J. (1982). SWAP—Strategies which affect programs: A framework for staff development. In J. Brown (Ed.), *Curriculum planning for young children* (pp. 246–254). Washington, DC: NAEYC.

Whitebook, M., & Morin, J. (1987). *Salaries, working conditions, and the teacher shortage* [Video]. Washington, DC: NAEYC.

Whitebook, M., Howes, C., & Phillips, D. (1989). *Who cares? Child care teachers and the quality of care in America: Executive summary.* Washington, DC: NAEYC.

Willer, B. (1987). *Quality, compensation, and affordability: An action kit.* Washington, DC: NAEYC.

Willer, B. (Ed.). (1990). *Reaching the full cost of quality in early childhood programs.* Washington, DC: NAEYC.

References

Jones, E., & Reynolds, G. (1992). *The play's the thing: Teachers' roles in children's play.* New York: Teachers College Press.

Nicholson, S. (1974). How not to cheat children: The theory of loose parts. In G. Coates (Ed.), *Alternate learning environments.* Stroudsburg, PA: PA: Dowden, Hutchinson and Ross.

Whitebook, M., Phillips, D., & Howes, C. (1989). *The National Child Care Staffing Study.* Oakland, CA: Child Care Employee Project.

> **To contact the author, write**
> Margie Carter, 3212 E. Terrace,
> Seattle, WA 98122.

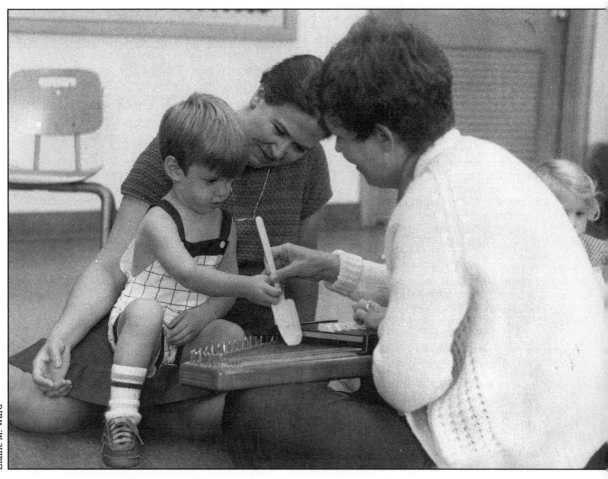

I n the Pasadena Partnership Project, college staff and school-district administrators designed a collaborative effort to improve quality in the district's prekindergarten programs. Faculty interest in issues of teacher growth and learning was an important component motivating active college participation in the project. The challenge of collaboration with school district administrators who had, of necessity, their own agendas created dynamic tension between the partners. Facilitators' advocacy for teacher choice and empowerment within these constraints led, over time, to mutual problem solving that benefited all of the participants and generated the conceptual framework for this book.

Chapter 4

Teachers Talking to Each Other: The Pasadena Partnership Project

Elizabeth Jones, Joyce Robinson, Diedra Miller, Richard Cohen, and Gretchen Reynolds

——————————— **Notes From the Storyteller*** ———————————

Telling It Like It Is

Washington Children's Center—Kathy Reisig, teacher; Caridad Bonilla, aide

The four-year-olds are very interested in hole punches these days. Several children are absorbed at a table with paper, hole punches, paste, scissors, and some other items, like buttons. For a while they were trying to figure out how to make buttons stick to paper. Kathy shows me two little papers Charles had produced (see p. 56). Then she points out the bulletin board. "Did you see Mrs. Bonilla's penguins?"

We admire the penguins together. Black and white penguin parts, big and little, orange beaks and feet (all skillfully cut by the adult), and assorted white shapes cut from styrofoam trays have been glued on blue construction paper. Children have chosen different combinations of shapes and sizes, and their inventions are lively and not all alike. Each child's name is clearly printed twice by Mrs. Bonilla, once on the picture and once with the child's words about the picture. Mrs. Bonilla is working in the afternoon these days, when there is relaxed time for her to sit at an outdoor table with interested children; she cuts, and they glue, and draw, and everybody talks together. Children who don't want to sit can ride off on bikes and come back later to join the conversation. It's a lot like a safe neighborhood with grandma watching out for children, working with her hands, and being present as a source of care and attention.

When parents and visitors see the evidence of children's work posted in the classroom, how will they know that the pasty little pictures children create on their own are just as important as the beautiful pictures co-created with a skilled and careful adult? Teachers can post signs that "tell it like it is," explaining briefly the process that led to each product. Visitors can read them, and children may like hearing them read as well.

The mother and the baby. Arts

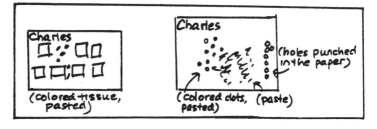

Here the storyteller is Betty Jones, resource team leader in a college–public school partnership, and this is a sample of the weekly newsletter in which classroom observations are shared with all of the district's prekindergarten teachers.

MRS. BONILLA AND THE CHILDREN CUT AND GLUED THESE PENGUINS.

CHARLES MADE HOLES WITH THE HOLE PUNCH.

HE MADE ONE HOLE.

HE MADE TWO HOLES.

HE MADE THREE HOLES.

HE MADE MORE AND MORE HOLES.

HE WORKED FOR A LONG TIME.

THEN HE PASTED THE HOLES ON THIS PAPER.

Each picture on the wall has its story; we can understand it better if we know something of that story. Each teacher has her story too; we can understand each other better if we know something of those stories. Mrs. Bonilla's schooling emphasized order and obedience and neat work, and these are values she continues to hold. Kathy has come to value most highly the work children do for themselves, but she is able to appreciate other staff members' values too.

In her recent in-service Bev Bos talked about risk taking. She commented on "the spiritual risk of getting to know other people—who they really are." The risk, I think, is that as we accept other people's differences from ourselves we necessarily become more open to other possibilities for our own growth as well, and less certain of who *we* really are.

Emergent curriculum is risky, too. It involves planning—and letting go of plans if something unpredicted but important happens. In teaching it is never possible to predict everything that will happen. Valuable curriculum emerges out of our goals for children's learning, out of children's interests, and out of teachers' interests as well.

—*Betty Jones, observer*

The setting

The Pasadena Partnership Project, which began in 1987, has involved faculty from Pacific Oaks College and Children's Programs collaborating with teaching staff in Pasadena Unified School District's (PUSD's) Children's Services Department, which administers both full-day children's centers and half-day state preschools serving income-eligible families. In this community of 120,000 in the Los Angeles metropolitan area, the majority of the low-income families are Latino and African American. Young children in preschool may speak English, Spanish, or any of the dozens of other languages found in this metropolis. Some of the preschool programs are Spanish bilingual.

Child care and preschool programs are located on elementary school (and one high school) sites and receive both state and local funding. The half-day preschools, for three- and four-year-olds, are free. In full-day care, fees are charged on a sliding scale, and care is provided both for three- and four-year-olds and for school-age children. California's child care centers date back to the the 1930s; the state took over after federal funding was discontinued at the end of World War II. State preschools began in the 1960s, when they were defined as compensatory education.

In Pasadena there are five full-day children's centers with separate classes for threes and fours; each class enrolls up to 18 children and is staffed by a teacher and morning and afternoon aides. The six half-day preschool teachers each have two classes, morning and afternoon, with an aide for each. The 16 teachers in these two programs have been the primary participants in the staff development activities of the partnership project. In some activities they have been joined by aides; children's center head teachers; school-age program staff; parents, staff and students from Pacific Oaks children's school; and staff from other programs in the Pasadena community. In the fifth year of the partnership, a training contract with Pasadena Head Start added in-service for some 50 Head Start staff as a partnership responsibility, involving both partnership staff and PUSD teachers in leadership roles.

Pacific Oaks College in Pasadena offers upper-division and graduate work in human development/early childhood education. Its faculty work in college and/or children's programs. The Children's School, with more than 200 children from birth to age eight, enrolls primarily families who can afford its tuition, while representing diverse racial and cultural backgrounds.

Several key players initiated the idea of a partnership. The school district's Adopt-a-School office—responsible for developing public/private partnerships, most of which provided materials and other curriculum resources—had approached Pacific Oaks. Joyce Robinson—a Pacific Oaks graduate, district teacher for some years, and now program coordinator for the district's Children's Services Division, was looking for ways to introduce more developmentally appropriate practice into long-established early childhood programs. In need of a support system and resources, she also looked to Pacific Oaks, not for "adoption," but for a mutual partnership in which Pacific Oaks and PUSD Children's Services would become resources for each other. Pacific Oaks Research Center, seeking funded projects, was aware of the Ford Foundation's interest in supporting educational partnerships with emphasis on staff development and dissemination of findings. Brainstorming between the two institutions began, with both administrators and teachers represented. Ford provided seed money and then a three-year grant.

The model was an emergent one, changing in response to the interests of participants and to our successes and failures in working together. During the pilot year we were able to agree that our focus would be on supporting staff to support children's play and language development. Play had not been a district value, but language development was, and we were clear about the linkage between them. Documentation of children's play could reinforce teachers' modification of their behavior in order to support play. A teacher empowerment model was necessary; if teachers were to support choice making by children, they would have to experience choice making themselves.

The original vision focused on interactions among teachers of children at Pacific

The partnership also received simultaneous and subsequent support from the ARCO Foundation (project evaluation), the Stuart and Irvine Foundations (parent support component), the Rockefeller Brothers Fund (career development), and the Hasbro Corporation (Head Start component). Grants to Children's Services under Title VII Bilingual Program and the state's literacy and nutrition programs added further resources, as did a grant from Roger Tory Peterson Foundation to develop a nature education curriculum. In the project's fifth year, State Preschool Expansion funds became available, and the number of preschool sites has tripled.

Oaks and in the school district, and a variety of exchanges took place in the early stages of the project. The project's major emphasis, however, has been staff development for the school district's teachers of young children.

Building a partnership: Who were the players?

The project employed a full-time coordinator and was overseen by a steering committee representing PUSD and Pacific Oaks. Classroom observations were made—as permitted or requested by teachers—by members of the Resource Support Team, several external facilitators. The persons initially active in this role were Betty Jones of Pacific Oaks faculty; Gretchen Reynolds, Pacific Oaks adjunct faculty; and Mel Lindsey, a consultant who knew the teachers through his work with them as a High/Scope trainer. Mel focused on planning environments with teachers; Gretchen and Betty observed children's play, took notes, and wrote a newsletter. Gretchen also offered video observations, as did Bill Smith, a video specialist. All of these people participated in the monthly in-services required of the school district's teachers, which proved an important way of building relationships. In the second and fifth years of the project, relationships were also built in a weekly seminar on play and language development and in biweekly seminars attended by PUSD teachers interested in working with adults in Head Start and other settings.

Gretchen and Betty had asked to be included in the project because of their interest in both play and teacher growth. Observers and writers, they had data collection in mind. Gretchen was able to sustain systematic observations for her dissertation research in a sample of classrooms in PUSD and Pacific Oaks, but observations for the partnership took their shape from our commitment to write a weekly newsletter and our wish to communicate our thinking about the importance of play while acknowledging and sharing interesting events from as many classrooms as possible. Gretchen and Betty also led the weekly seminar on play and language development, in which regulars (teachers and Pacific Oaks students) and visitors were encouraged to talk about whatever interested them. Teachers' concerns about power and communication sometimes took precedence over their interest in children's play. We tried, not always successfully, to be supportive without taking sides.

If we all have choices and we each have our own agendas, we need to learn to dance together without tromping too hard on each other's toes. There were many players in the partnership, and multiple lines of communication and understanding had to be established. As administrators and facilitators observed and inter-

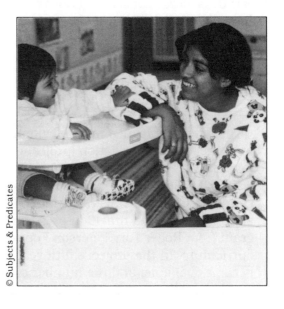

© Subjects & Predicates

> Like teaching, working in partnership is an emergent process. Some parts of the original design prove not to work. Other parts develop a life of their own, serendipitously becoming the partnership's most significant accomplishments.
>
> Each member of the team has her own agenda, often hidden, to which others must learn to accommodate. If all team members become co-learners, continuing partnership is possible and even exhilarating, although never tension free.

acted with each other, we grew in mutual understanding and respect. As participation in out-of-town conferences brought teachers into informal contact with administrators and college faculty, everyone had opportunities to share planning, anxieties, and the sense of a job well done.

Richard Cohen, who joined the partnership as project evaluator, stayed on as Pacific Oaks research director, contributing his experience in teaching young children, ethnographic research, relationship building, and community sings with his guitar. Diedra Miller, who became project coordinator in the third year of the partnership, brought clarity of vision, administrative experience, and endless reserves of support for everyone. Her background with Head Start provided useful liaison when the partnership expanded to include Pasadena Head Start. The partnership faces new challenges as we expand our collaboration with the school district to include support for more developmentally appropriate practice in kindergarten and primary grades. Writing the proposal for support for this new venture, we were pleased to discover our agreement on replicating, with a new group of teachers, the staff development strategies that had evolved in our preschool work.

During the project, definitions of roles and responsibilities at all levels continued to emerge as we experienced what worked and what didn't. Except for in-services and an evaluation component, teacher participation was defined as voluntary. The project design stated our expectation that some teachers would be active participants, some moderately active, and some remain on the periphery. That expectation has proved true, as has our prediction that, over time, the number of active participants would increase. Each new choice, we have found, "hooks" a few more teachers; so does an atmosphere in which being "hooked" is acceptable, even the norm. As teachers of young children, we haven't been surprised by this discovery. By the end of the third year, all but one teacher had taken advantage of at least one of the choices available; by the end of the fourth year, all of the teachers had.

Staff development strategies: Choices available to teachers

Classroom observations

At first we confidently passed around a sign-up sheet at in-services, asking, Would you like an observer in your classroom? That approach gained response only from a few teachers interested in environmental assessment with Mel and from a few friendly and confident souls who said, "Sure, any time." These gave us starting points. Later we approached other teachers with "Would you mind if I visited? I'm watching children's play." Some agreed to let us observe; a few didn't. Their confidence was not helped by the fact that shortly after we had assured teachers that we would visit only if welcome and that we would be observing *children*, the project's evaluation component began with required classroom visits to gather baseline data on *teacher* behavior. A few teachers flatly refused to admit the evaluation observer, and those of us more interested in teacher empowerment than in evaluation were pleased by their assertiveness. Prompt formation of an evaluation task force that included teachers reduced their opposition, however; and the significant quantitative changes shown in these systematic observations proved important in reporting to funders, the school district, and the professional community.

Stories selected from informal observations were shared in conversations with and written notes to teachers, a weekly or biweekly project newsletter featuring observations from one or more classrooms (with teacher permission), videotapes (which were given to teachers for their private viewing or discussed with the observer at the teacher's request), plan drawings for environmental changes, and storytelling at in-services by teachers or by others with the teachers' permission.

Seminars: Teachers as researchers

During the second year a weekly afternoon Research Seminar: Play and Language Development, co-led by Betty and Gretchen, was attended regularly by a group of PUSD teachers and aides and Pacific Oaks college students, and irregu-

larly by other teachers and people with project connections. Its content emerged out of all of our observations, questions, and concerns. This seminar was discontinued in the third year when preschool staff had afternoon sessions added to their teaching load. In the fifth year, when our relationship with Head Start began, we instituted a Working with Adults seminar, meeting biweekly in the evenings, for teachers interested in moving into mentor relationships. This seminar is described on page 63 under "Mentor Teaching."

Visiting between classrooms

Some teachers, both in the district and in Pacific Oaks Children's School, arranged visits to each other's classrooms or shared field trips. Pacific Oaks' art studio and artist-in-residence were a resource for a number of teachers and children from the district.

Task force decision making

Teachers gained opportunities to engage in decision making at the project and district levels through several task forces established during the project (and meeting during teachers' work time, with substitutes provided). An evaluation task force was begun in direct response to teacher complaints about the intrusion of project evaluation procedures. Additional task forces worked on selecting children's books for classrooms, developing a parent support program, and planning presentations at early childhood conferences.

Conference presentations

Each year we have scheduled conference presentations at state and national AEYC conferences and have invited teachers to apply to participate. This has proved a highly motivating and affirming experience for teachers. Some have gone on to get involved in other conferences as well; they are seeing themselves as professionals with knowledge to share.

In-service presentations

Although the monthly in-service was a district requirement throughout the project, attendance and involvement increased significantly from year to year. From the earlier training-by-expert model, in-services were restructured to encourage teacher presentations and peer dialogue. A facilitator, focusing the topic, created opportunities for teachers to describe related classroom activities they have found successful. Teachers who chose to enroll for Pacific Oaks Extension credit were expected to present a project; some others volunteered to participate. Dramatic-play kits, bulletin boards, story stretchers, field trips, and a wide range of classroom activities have been shared among teaching staff. Both teachers and aides have gained notably in confidence in talking to a group of peers and in appreciation of the quality of their own professional practice.

College enrollment

A grant from the Rockefeller Brothers Fund has enabled Pacific Oaks College to offer career-incentive opportunities to PUSD staff involved in the project. A dozen teachers and aides have entered part-time bachelor's, master's, and credential programs in early childhood education.

Mentor teaching

Some of the experienced teachers empowered by this variety of experiences have expressed interest in becoming external facilitators themselves. They now constitute a resource support team

available to Head Start teaching staff under a recent contract with Pasadena Head Start, the newest member of the partnership. They have taken a leadership role in Head Start in-services and have begun exchange visiting. The biweekly Working with Adults seminar enables teachers to share stories and questions and to build a mutual support network. Facilitation for that seminar has been provided by Betty Jones, Diedra Miller, and Mary Beth Lakin, another Pacific Oaks faculty member who now has PUSD staff in some of her college classes.

In the implementation of a facilitation model, size is important; the model won't work on an impersonal scale. To extend the model to a Head Start program serving twice as many children in 25 classrooms, extension of the resource support pool to draw on teacher-peer leadership is both necessary and desirable.

Sources of success and conflict

The success of this choice-based, emergent model in this setting has depended on (1) a stable teaching staff coming from a baseline of training in developmentally appropriate curriculum, and (2) supervisory staff who are willing and able to support, albeit with some reservations at times, teacher growth in autonomy.

Baseline competence

Choice presupposes baseline competence. For new or borderline teaching staff, clear requirements and a training plan are the first priority. *Training*, unlike facilitation, sets specific goals for teacher behavior, and teachers are held accountable for meeting those goals.

Pasadena Children's Services teaching staff is exceptionally stable, thanks to relatively high (for early childhood education) wages and benefits. Most teachers have been with the program for 5 to 15 years and have been through several training plans, most recently (just before the partnership began) the High/Scope curriculum. This model emphasizes the development of classroom learning environments that support play; it was selected by supervisory staff to promote program development in this direction. While it offers a clear framework for teacher performance, it is an open framework, necessitating teacher inventiveness within its perimeters; thus it is compatible with the choosing and questioning inherent in a facilitative model.

Encouraging disequilibrium

Teachers who have mastered the basic elements of such a curriculum are ready to experience the creative tension of raising questions about it and inventing variations reflecting their own unique styles. Facilitators in this project raised questions with teachers as a matter of strategy and, as trust was established, out of their own thinking, as well. Both Betty and Gretchen had doubts about the appropriateness of several aspects of High/Scope and mentioned them on occasion. A teacher who refused classroom visits for the first two years and later became an enthusiastic project participant, making changes in her classroom that went beyond the High/Scope structure, talked in a conference presentation about her earlier perceptions of the project: "We'd been told all the things we were supposed to do, and there were you folks saying something different, and there was no way I was going to deal with that. I know who pays my salary."

In a school system there are structural constraints that limit the autonomy of supervisors as well as teachers. Shifting enrollments and budget limitations threaten teachers' job security some years, introducing, if not fear of actual job loss, at least uncertainty about one's placement for the following year. Transfers from one site to another happened to some staff every year. Bilingual funding shifted priorities, giving Spanish-speaking teachers precedence in some instances over teachers with greater seniority. Before the third year of the project, the job of preschool teacher was redefined to include both morning and afternoon sessions (previously it was a six-hour job, with one session's teaching plus preparation time); there was considerable moving of teachers, and we gave up our weekly afternoon seminar, which preschool teachers had previously been free to attend.

Such changes create anxiety. Anxious teachers often devote less energy to curriculum than to worry about the future and complaints about administrators. An external facilitator, outside the loop but available to listen sympathetically, may hear a good many complaints about the frustrations in teachers' work settings. If the facilitator says, "What could you do about that?" and supports teachers' initiative in requesting meetings with supervisors, she risks becoming a troublemaker—if supervisors are experiencing their own anxieties and are demanding loyalty, not challenge. We learned about these risks by taking them and by struggling through the consequences together.

Constructive problem solving and supervisory support

We all had some uneasy moments. Several factors made it possible to move beyond these moments: teacher initiative in problem solving, the function of the project steering committee in providing external facilitation for supervisors, and supervisors' genuine commitment to teacher growth.

When staff is relatively stable and baseline competence is established, facilitators can introduce healthy disequilibrium by

1. observing individual differences among children in their responses to curriculum and sharing observations with teachers;

2. viewing teachers as co-researchers in an ethnographic mode and asking genuine questions—Why do you do that?;

3. encouraging teachers to talk with each other about children, curriculum, and strategies for change;

4. asking, What would happen to you if you did/didn't do that? and encouraging teachers to take individual and collective action on their concerns;

5. encouraging teachers to seek further professional development;

6. encouraging teachers to take leadership roles—articulating what they do and why—in in-services, workshops, conferences, and mentor relationships; and

7. giving teachers choices about their participation at every level of staff-development activities.

A crucial contribution to shared problem solving was made by a teacher who had one day used the play and language seminar to vent some of her system complaints. Shortly afterward, she explained at the next in-service, she had suddenly thought, If I have complaints, it's my responsibility to think of something to do about them. And so she arrived at the in-service with a suggestion box that she had asked the children in her class to decorate "for all the teachers." "This is for us," she explained. "I'll bring it to every meeting. And I'm giving a party and you're all invited and it will be there too. Put any suggestions or complaints you have in the box, and I hope somebody will do something about them."

"I will," the project evaluator volunteered. "I'll type them up and give everyone a copy. And we'll do our best to see that each one is followed up."

"What if someone recognizes our handwriting?" asked a teacher. It was clear that she wasn't kidding.

In Los Angeles in the spring of 1992, many people acted out their anger over injustice. There are many diverse peoples living together in this city, and some of them have trouble gaining self-respect or hope for the future. Their stories aren't taken seriously by people in power. You can't *train* teachers to create riot curriculum; riots aren't in the lesson plan. But in classroom after classroom of teachers with whom we've been working, riot curriculum emerged because it was part of those teachers' and children's stories. If we share our stories, perhaps we can learn to problem-solve together in classrooms and in our communities (Jones, 1992; see also p. 67, this volume).

"Print, if you like," said the evaluator, "but I really don't know your handwriting, and I promise you no one else will see it."

The party took place, and many people came. The suggestion box was there, and not all of the conversation at the party was unrelated to work issues. And then another teacher gave another party. The suggestion box lasted for the rest of the school year and then faded away; people had become more at ease at speaking up, and there was less to complain about. Suggestions, faithfully transcribed and distributed, ranged from play dough recipes to the resentment about the evaluation procedure that led to teacher inclusion in an evaluation task force and, shortly thereafter, some procedural changes. It was clear to teachers that their voices were being heard, and they continued to speak up. They also found increasing energy to devote to curriculum and children.

Administrators often lack peers to talk to. And in supervisory positions in a larger system, they are under pressure from both directions—those whom they supervise and *their* supervisors. Participation in a small project-steering committee that meets weekly and whose other members are not school district employees offers facilitative relationships to the supervisor—and a place to complain about the behavior of resource support team members who work directly with teachers (and are not members of the steering committee). Tolerance and confrontation are alternative follow-up strategies, and both were employed. Over time, increasing trust was built, and both became less necessary.

Supervisors directly responsible for teacher performance have good reason to be skeptical of the behavior of so-called facilitators, who have little to lose by raising questions. The facilitator's role is a tricky one. She is working to empower teachers, to increase their autonomy and capacity for decision making both in their classrooms and in the larger system. To do so without undermining supervisors or training goals requires the capacity to see both sides, to pay attention when confronted, and to build and maintain trust with supervisors as well as teachers. Things have not been all smooth sailing in the partnership; there have been substantial issues to work through. This would not have been possible if supervisors were too vulnerable or too rigid and did not share the goal of increasing staff autonomy at some level.

Empowering teachers

The last partnership newsletter of the 1991–92 school year, which describes teachers' contributions at an in-service, reflects teachers' growth in knowledge, leadership, and trust.

When the project began teachers who shared ideas and materials did so only with their close friends; the openness reflected at the in-service described in the newsletter on pages 67 to 69 did not exist. Teachers had fewer opportunities to get to know each other, and when they came together in a group, they were often listening rather than sharing. Joyce Robinson was able to continue her weekly meeting with the preschool teachers even when afternoon classes were added by asking staff how it could be done. Their collaborative decision was to make each Wednesday morning a combined day for morning and afternoon children; but child care teachers, who need substitutes to enable them to leave the classroom, were included only in the High/Scope in-services and later in the monthly partnership in-services. In the bureaucratic thicket of a city school district, making time for staff development is no small accomplishment.

Opportunities to share ideas informally have led to remarkable growth in teachers' leadership skills. Child care teacher Rosi

Volume 4, No. 14 June 15, 1992

TELLING OUR STORIES

For teachers, it's different to be told by an official expert, "This is what you should do in your classroom," than to be told by a friend, "This is what I did in my classroom." Experts are sometimes wrong, but everyone's story is true; it is what happened for a teacher and children, and another teacher can choose whether to try the idea herself. Piaget has pointed out that children construct knowledge more solidly in dialogue with a peer than in discussion with a teacher. That's because you can argue with your friend, knowing that your understanding is probably as good as hers—but your teacher knows everything.

In-services for teachers often rely on the transmission of expertise by outsiders. Partnership in-services have become mostly storytelling by insiders, from which we all keep learning. Here are some of the important stories teachers told at the May in-service.

* * *

Emergent curriculum: The riots

The Los Angeles riots had both emotional and physical impact on the three- and four-year-olds we teach. Children were acting out their feelings with fists and attacks— but sensitive teachers found ways to help children use their words to express their fears.

"At first I thought they weren't affected. They said nothing about it for two days," said Mamie. But when she brought a microphone to circle time and invited children to do "interviews," they went on all morning "with all this stuff on killing and burning—from three-year-olds! It shocked me," said Mamie.

At Willard, Sue's threes wouldn't talk about it at circle time, and drawing didn't do it either. So Sue brought her tape recorder and told the children she was making a newspaper. "Know what a newspaper is? It's everyone's stories. Can you tell me your stories about what's been happening in Los Angeles?" Children went off by themselves so they wouldn't be heard and talked to the recorder. Sue transcribed their stories, which are full of their fears. She plans to invite children to talk about it again, later, to see if anything has changed for them.

Next door, Joyce invited her fours to draw and dictate stories. She made their pictures and stories into a book: *A Child's View of the LA Riots.* "The police were chasing Rodney King." "Grandma's house is on fire. The policeman is on fire." "They beat Rodney King. Why do they only beat Black people?"

* * *

You're my friend

Mainstreaming children with special needs at Roosevelt, which began on a small scale in Jackie's classroom, has expanded into contacts among all the children in both state preschool and special-needs preschools. "We're putting them all together," Mamie and Jackie explained. A doll named Sarah, who has crutches, has helped Mamie's children deal with their anxieties about differences: "They treat her like a person. And they see I'm not afraid, and now they're not." Shared circle time, with children in partners, focuses on being friends: I like me, I like you. And children are becoming friends, seeking each other on the playground and caring for each other, touching, holding hands, straightening glasses, and cheering new accomplishments.

Joyce Robinson commented that children with special needs often don't have much opportunity to be independent and make choices. Their interactions with normal children challenge both them and their teachers to discover what they can do. "Stand up, boy. She didn't say siddown!" said a child to Johnny during a group activity. Johnny can't stand up, but he can get himself around and is keeping up with the rest of the children.

"We're a good teaching team," said Mamie to Jackie. And antibias curriculum is alive and well at Roosevelt.

* * *

Bookmaking—and watching children grow

At Hodges, Rosi knows that dictating stories is one of the things children do in order to learn to read and write, and she has invented a variety of strategies to encourage them. "Do you have a story you want to tell today?" she asks, as she goes around with a clipboard. "How about looking at these animal pictures; what can you say about them?" "Want to make a pop-up book?" "Want to add a page to our Dinosaur Book?" A child's collection of stories becomes a beautifully bound book. Rosi said about Christopher's, "When we went to the library, I snuck in *Christopher Climbs a Tree* for the librarian to read to the children. When she announced it, I thought Christopher was going to pass out. He was so pleased." And everyone went back to school wanting to make books. "I can't bind them fast enough," said Rosi.

"All of us are supposed to be keeping a portfolio on the children," explained Rosi, showing us Miguel's portfolio as a vivid record of his growth, over the year, in drawing, planning, writing, and storytelling. His story of *Miguel and Sticky Bear*, with clear sequence and wonderful dialogue, reminded us all of the wonder of children's growth, and our "Oohs" filled the room.

What's in the bathtub?

If a teacher reads stories in one language, how can she help the children who don't speak that language understand? Georgina treated us to a Spanish reading, acting out the story with props. "Chinchinchirina!! Que hay en la tina?"

Risk taking: Trying new things

At Washington, Kathy has been consciously risk taking in lots of different ways. She described her staff's varied approaches to artwork with children and her own decision to concentrate on open-ended exploration of materials. They have been eagerly inventing with scrap materials, and "What you see on my lesson plan may not be what we do," as creativity takes over. To children's posted work she adds their Polaroid pictures and a list of the materials used, to interpret the process to parents. Glue and tape are essentials, but, "I'm blessed with a head teacher who values these things. If we use a whole roll of tape, it's OK." Children do their share; they set up the art area all by themselves. "They even fill the glue bottles." "Ooh," said several teachers.

Connie has expanded her dramatic-play kits—carefully organized collections of resources related to field trips her children at Muir take. She offers to loan them to anyone interested—and already has. "I feel a little selfish because this year I did something for me," she began. "Whoops," burst in Georgina. "You find a Key Experience for that, no problem!"

And Jackie at Jefferson has been collecting great resources, too; a tornado tube— "This is a blast!"—a ball and bat, a birthday kit, and inexpensive juicers in which each child made his/her own cup of orange juice. She had fun telling us about them, too. Joyce Robinson spoke about her administrative risk taking, too. We've all come a long way in trusting each other.

—*Betty Jones, observer*

Pollard has presented her bookmaking workshop to all Head Start staff as well as to her PUSD colleagues, copresented at several national conferences, supervised Pacific Oaks practicum students, and won a merit scholarship as she completes her M.A. and teaching credential through the partnership's Success program. With Sue Bush and Connie Wortham, Rosi also participated in Louise Derman-Sparks' ongoing antibias seminar for community teachers. Sue joined a Pacific Oaks master teacher in developing and implementing a nature education curriculum (for the Roger Tory Peterson Foundation) and has in-serviced other teachers in the program nationally as well as at home. Sue and her teaching partner, Joyce Mortara, deciding they needed daily planning time together, asked their head teacher to start covering for them at naptime, and she agreed.

Michaelyn Straub

Half of the 16 teachers have copresented at state and national conferences, representing not only the partnership but also the bilingual program and the antibias task force. Their adventures were reported to their colleagues at in-services and, on one occasion, were listened to with increasing interest by teachers visiting from another agency. A round-the-group structure introduced by the facilitator asked each person to tell us, Why did/ didn't you go to the conference? If you did, tell us, "Fortunately..." and "Unfortunately..." about your good and bad experiences there. The ensuing conversation became exceedingly lively, and our visitors made comments like "We didn't go 'cause no one told us about it" and "Do you always have this much fun at in-services? All we do at ours is listen." Teachers advised them to start questioning their director. "But be careful. You'll get in trouble if you start risk taking. We did," said one teacher with a grin. "But it's worth it."

Half of the teachers have offered leadership at Head Start in-services. At the first partnership in-service with Head Start, district teachers talked about their experiences and then led small group discussions on topics of their (and Head Start staff's) choice. The level of enthusiastic interaction and questioning was high, with little of the suspicion and standoffishness we had experienced in our early district in-services. Teachers-talking-to-teachers is a different experience from experts-talking-to-teachers; after all, they teach children every day, too. Self-selected teachers have participated in a biweekly seminar, Working with Adults, in order to support their developing mentorships with Head Start teachers. "But don't call us mentors," they protested. "That makes us sound like experts. We're...what? Friends. Buddies. Sisters." This seminar gives Pacific Oaks College credit, useful to the group of district staff who have enrolled for degrees under the Success program, advised by Betty Jones and Diedra Miller.

The partnership has become a natural support network on several occasions when district changes in personnel and program threatened teachers' familiar roles and responsibilities. At meetings teachers made it clear, even when the meeting was ostensibly to plan a conference presentation, that their job agenda took precedence. This happened in the project's fifth year, when a plan for merging state preschools with the district's K–4 program was announced in the newspaper by the associate superintendent. This was news to the teachers, who were especially incensed by his reported remarks that K–4, staffed by credentialed teachers, was a superior program. The preschool teachers promptly demanded a meeting with the administrator and met with their union representative. Eventually they participated with K–4 teachers in a two-day retreat for planning and problem solving. The retreat was initiated by Joyce Robinson, facilitated by a Pacific Oaks faculty member not previously involved with the partnership, and hosted by the college. Partner-

---

In Pasadena in 1989–92 all of these programs served three- and four-year-olds from low-income families:
• Pasadena Head Start, with 25 classrooms at four sites (an independent agency);
• Foothill Area Community Service State Preschool, with three classrooms at two sites (an independent agency);
• PUSD (school district) state preschools, with six classrooms at four sites;
• PUSD children's centers (full-day care), with 10 classrooms at five sites; and
• PUSD K–4 program, a three-year, foundation-initiated and -funded project with a classroom in each of the district's 19 elementary schools. Teachers held elementary credentials and reported to the principal.

* * *

Except for children's centers, all programs offer half-day morning and afternoon classes. Except for teachers of K–4, teachers hold, not elementary credentials, but children's center permits. Head Start teachers may have either a permit or a CDA.

The expected end in 1992 of foundation support for K–4 coincided with the availability of state preschool expansion grants. In the fall of 1992, the two programs merged—with limited continuation of foundation funding supplementing state funding—into 22 classrooms under the supervision of the elementary principals. A plan to increase class size from 15 or 16 to 24—to be staffed by a team including a credentialed teacher, two permit teachers, and an aide—fell victim to last-minute budget cuts, and in 1992–93 credentialed and permit teachers have comparable responsibilities with a large pay differential. This change has threatened permit teachers' accustomed autonomy in their classrooms and ignored their much-longer experience in teaching at the preschool level, as well as creating site changes and a host of interpersonal unknowns. The major issues of professional certification that divide early childhood education are alive and well in Pasadena, creating new tensions and new challenges.

ship staff and Children's Services administrators were full participants in the two-day process.

What was taught, what was learned, and what are the implications?

Observation of children is a solid, shared focus for building relationships with teachers.

Giving teachers choices among resources builds feeling of empowerment.

Although no plan will have an impact on all staff members, the more choices given, the more staff who will be "hooked" into investing energy in their own growth.

A good plan is emergent, just as a good curriculum is. It is impossible to predict which choices will be most effective or what staff agendas will be introduced along the way by increasingly empowered teachers.

Maslow's hierarchy of needs, in which needs for safety and belonging must be met before needs for mastery and competence can take priority, is a good predictor of teacher involvement in staff development (1970). Teachers with personal or job security needs aren't free to focus on learning more about children. Some (but not all) veteran teachers are truly tired (as one of them mentioned, 247 days a year, eight hours a day, for 15 years is a lot of time with children); they welcome sympathy, but not challenge.

In some bureaucracies, mediocrity without making waves is the desired norm. Not all administrators support the risk taking that accompanies change; both those who do and facilitators promoting change need to stay alert to this fact.

As relationships are built and interesting things happen, facilitators may experience a halo effect, as teachers begin attributing everything good to them. It would be easy for administrators to resent this phenomenon.

Empowered teachers can move beyond academic fears to become increasingly confident degree candidates, provided their college classes enable them to draw on their work experience in demonstrating competence.

Trust building and change take time, measured in years. There is no quick fix.

For further information

Carter, M., Jones, E., & Lakin, M.B. (1991). *Ideas for staff development.* Occasional paper. Pasadena, CA: Pacific Oaks College. 22 pp. $1.75.

Cohen, R., Jones, E., Miller, D., Reynolds, G., & Robinson, J. (1991). *How do you grow teachers? The Pasadena Partnership Project.* Occasional paper. Pasadena, CA: Pacific Oaks College. 14 pp. $1.75.

Jones, E. (1989, December). Inviting children into the fun: Providing enough activity choices outdoors. *Child Care Information Exchange, 70.*

Jones, E. (1990). Playing is my job. *Thrust for Educational Leadership, 20*(2), 10–13.

Jones, E. (1992, June). *Teaching adults to teach young children.* Paper presented at the first annual conference of NAEYC's National Institute for Early Childhood Professional Development, Los Angeles, CA. (available from the author)

Jones, E. (1993, January/February). The play's the thing: Styles of playfulness. *Child Care Information Exchange, 89,* 28–30.

Jones, E., & Reynolds, G. (1988–1992). *Observation notes: Play and language development.* The newsletter of the Partnership Project. Pacific Oaks College/ Pasadena Unified School District: Vols. 1–4. Occasional papers. Pasadena, CA: Pacific Oaks College. Vol. 1, $4.95; other vols., $3.50.

Jones, E., & Reynolds, G. (1992). *The play's the thing: Teachers' roles in children's play.* New York: Teachers College Press.

Reynolds, G. (1991). *The role of pretend play in the development of master players.* Unpublished doctoral dissertation, Claremont Graduate School, Claremont, CA.

Sofio, M. (1992). *Dialogue: An essential component of an effective training model.*

Unpublished master's thesis, Pacific Oaks College, Pasadena, CA.

Villarino, G., as told to Jones, E. (in press). What goes up on the classroom walls—and why? *Young Children, 48*(4).

Other suggested readings

Cambourne, B. (1987). Language, learning and literacy. In A. Butler & J. Turbill (Eds.), *Toward a reading-writing classroom* (pp. 5–9). Portsmouth, NH: Heinemann.

Dyson, A.H. (1990). Research in review. Symbol makers, symbol weavers: How children link play, pictures, and print. *Young Children, 45*(2), 50–57.

Elbow, P. (1990). *Embracing contraries: Explorations in learning and teaching.* New York: Oxford University Press.

Greenman, J. (1989, October). Diversity and conflict: The whole world will never sing in perfect harmony. *Child Care Information Exchange, 69,* 11–13.

Heath, S.B. (1983). *Ways with words: Language, life and work in communities and classrooms.* Cambridge: Cambridge University Press.

Jones, E. (Ed.). (1988). *Reading, writing and talking with four, five and six year olds.* Pasadena, CA: Pacific Oaks College.

Jones, E. (1991). Do ECE people really agree? Or are we just agreeable? *Young Children, 46*(4), 59–61.

Kuschner, D. (1989). "Put your name on your painting, but . . . the blocks go back on the shelves." *Young Children, 45*(1), 49–56.

Mills, H., & Clyde, J.A. (1991). Children's success as readers and writers: It's the teacher's beliefs that make the difference. *Young Children, 46*(2), 54–59.

Sarason, S.B. (1982). *The culture of the school and the problem of change.* Boston: Allyn & Bacon.

Van Hoorn, J., Nourot, P., Scales, B., & Alward, K. (1993). *Play at the center of the curriculum.* New York: Merrill/Macmillan.

Reference

Maslow, A. (1970). *Motivation and personality.* New York: Harper.

To contact the authors, write Research Center, Pacific Oaks College, 714 W. California Blvd., Pasadena, CA 91105.

© Carolyn Kozo

I n the following account of school change through a bilingual grant, we remain in the public school context but move from prekindergarten to the "real world" of the elementary school— in this case, a single primary school with a visionary principal. Joan Hillard collaborated with a resource teacher and a consultant to create a more developmentally appropriate program in kindergarten and first and second grades. Working from a project grant she had written and confident enough to regard teacher resistance as a source of energy in the change process, Joan used report card revision as a focusing task to empower teachers as observers of children and advocates for developmentally appropriate practice.

Chapter 5
Change Making in a Primary School: Soledad, California

Jane Meade-Roberts, Elizabeth Jones, and Joan Hillard

—————————— **Notes From the Storyteller*** ——————————

First grade

Laura never said a word at teachers' meetings, but in her first grade classroom—a no-nonsense, "let's get to work" place—she was clear and confident. Her own history of growing up in Soledad and her fluency in Spanish gave her immediate rapport with the children and with their parents.

She didn't invite me to visit her classroom, but she was gracious when I asked if I could come in for a while. This morning a spelling test was in progress. When it was over and papers were being passed in, to my surprise and without my notic-

ing quite how it happened, the room suddenly became a free-choice, activity-centers place. Out from somewhere came paper and markers, Lincoln logs, Barbies, a jump rope, a small trampoline, picture books—and play and spontaneous language took over. Jump-rope rhymes were chanted in both English and Spanish. Laura was reading and talking about books with several children. Children were busy and self-directed; and when cleanup time came, they returned things to their places as efficiently as they'd gotten them out.

"That was wonderful," I said to Laura as the children went out to recess. "They're so competent and cooperative. And this was really language arts, too, with all that conversation in two languages."

Here the storyteller is Betty Jones, a visiting consultant to San Vicente School, describing two of her conversations with teachers at the school.

Laura was a bit apologetic; she hadn't been expecting approval for just letting children play. "They worked so well at spelling," she explained, "that I thought they needed a reward. We do that sometimes."

"It was lovely to watch," I said. "I'm glad I came in just now. It makes such a nice balance in children's day, between work you ask them to do and choices they make for themselves.

"How is the Spanish language arts going?" I added, as we walked toward the teachers' room.

"You know, I didn't think we should be doing that, teaching reading in Spanish," she reminded me. "They have to learn English, right? But I'm doing it because they said we had to. And I think I'm changing my mind. You know Amelia? She's only been taught to read in Spanish, but today when we were looking at those books, she picked up one in English and started reading it to me. I wonder how she can do that?"

"I'm so glad you told me," I said happily. "That's how the theory says it's supposed to work, and I believe it does, but I've never been quite sure. You're gathering data to support it."

Laura's own Spanish-speaking family did their best to speak English to their children at home; they wanted the children to succeed in an English-speaking society. Few Soledad children grow up to be professionals, but Laura did; apparently the strategy worked. Laura is now embarrassed by her limited literacy in Spanish, however, since her knowledge of the language has become an important tool in her teaching, and she keeps a low profile as a Latina in a school where teachers are mostly Anglo (although aides, children, and parents are mostly Latino). Through professional challenges and her own direct experience she is developing a more complex view of language learning in a stratified society and of ways in which she can help children grow up with greater pride in who they are and with bicultural competence in a changing society.

Kindergarten

Anne and I have worked happily together for several years. When we first met she was teaching kindergarten as she'd been taught to teach, rotating small groups of children every 15 minutes through four "stations"—math activities, Spanish reading readiness, English reading readiness, and large-muscle activities. As I observed she was enthusiastically taking children through the textbook activities prescribed in the teacher's guide, focusing their discussion of pictures while staying open to some of their discoveries. "How many windows do you see in this picture?" she asked. "Let's count them together. One, two..." "Twenty-two!" announced the math whiz of the group. "Really?" Anne asked with great interest. "The book I'm reading says eleven. Let's see how you got twenty-two...Oh, I see. They're double windows, aren't they, and so you could count them both ways. . . . "

Anne's teaching partner was working with attribute blocks during this same period. Each child in her small group got a collection of blocks and waited for a turn to sort them in response to the teacher's questions. Fifteen minutes was up, I noticed, before everyone got a turn. Don't they mind? I wondered as I watched them file docilely on to the next station. I'd mind if I were five years old.

Anne invited me to sit with her at lunch in the teachers' room and asked what I'd seen. I mentioned how much I'd liked her response to the answer, "Twenty-two."— "You're really listening to children and not just reinforcing one right answer. That encourages them to observe carefully and think for themselves." Then I asked a genuine question—carefully, because I hadn't known Anne very long and I didn't want her to think I was criticizing: "Do you find that the 15-minute rotation gives children enough time at each activity?"

Anne heard it as a genuine question, and she thought about it. "Why, yes; but I'm only doing language arts with each small group; I don't know what's happening in the others. Why did you ask?" I explained what I'd seen with the attribute blocks. "Oh..." Anne said thoughtfully.

This conversation, Anne's own experience with choice making at an in-service (see below), the availability of new materials purchased under a Title VII grant, and encouragement from the teacher in the room next door (Jane Meade-Roberts, also hired under the grant) all led Anne to make radical changes in her classroom structure. Over the next year she gave up station rotation in favor of a long choice time, expanded the choice of centers outdoors as well as indoors, and worked out a team arrangement whereby teachers and aides from two adjacent classrooms shared responsibility for setting up learning centers in the patio area and supervising any children who were outside. She found these changes exciting and occasionally scary—was she teaching the children what they needed to know?

She and I were both reassured one morning when one of the outdoor activities was finger painting. It was an often-available choice, and children managed it themselves, putting on aprons, swirling paint around on a tabletop, and washing their hands in a convenient bucket. Adults were available with paper to make a print if there was a creation to be saved before more swirling went on. I enjoy watching children being competent and responsible, and I was enjoying watching these children, when I noticed, "Anne, LOOK. They're writing their names in the finger paint! Take a picture or make a print or something, so you can reassure parents you really are teaching writing." She shared my delight, and she did just that.

—*Betty Jones*

The setting

San Vicente School, where Laura and Anne were teaching, enrolls all of the K–1–2 children (600 to 800 of them) in Soledad, a predominantly Latino agricultural community in California's Salinas Valley. Third and fourth graders go to Gabilan School, fifth to eighth graders to Main Street; high school is in a neighboring community.

The majority of children enter school with little or no English proficiency, and instruction in English as a second language has been provided through migrant education and other funding; however, the superintendent for many years opposed bilingual education. It was not until the early 1980s, when he retired, that an opportunity arose to write a Title VII bilingual program grant to support changes in early childhood education in Soledad.

Joan Hillard, then the district's early childhood curriculum supervisor, coauthored the grant. In the year in which it was funded, she became principal of San Vicente School.

Building a partnership

In the partnership that developed, Joan Hillard as principal; Jane Meade-Roberts, teaching preschool at San Vicente under the Title VII grant; and Betty Jones, hired as a consultant from the faculty of Pacific Oaks College, were the principal players. As the project continued, some of the teachers chose to become active partners, too.

Joan had background as a teacher and a supervisor and solid understanding of theory in early childhood education. Her contribution to the writing of the Title VII grant ensured that it addressed developmentally appropriate practice as well as bilingual education. It included (1) a Spanish-immersion preschool for Spanish-speaking four- and five-year-olds, (2) a first grade readiness checklist for use by kindergarten teachers, (3) staff development, (4) purchase of developmentally appropriate materials, and (5) bilingual support staff.

Sharing responsibility was both a strategy and an intended outcome of the project. In her authority role as administrator, Joan had the power to be a fixer upper, as far as she was able. She was challenged to try to gain teachers' trust so that she could be facilitative as well as directive. In the process of doing so, she delegated many tasks to teachers. And she hired an experienced teacher with no history in the school or community for the new preschool, to whom she assigned responsibilities for staff development and in whom she had an ally who could, in turn, work with other teachers as their peer.

Jane Meade-Roberts had been a bilingual teacher in Los Angeles before earning her M.A. in human development at Pacific Oaks College and going on to further graduate work with Constance Kamii in Chicago. She brought to her new position at San Vicente her knowledge of developmental theory and her commitment to autonomy as the aim of education for both children and adults. In her first year she nevertheless experienced stress:

> My previous teaching experience was in bilingual classrooms, and I am a certified bilingual teacher, but I am not a native Spanish speaker, and at first I found it exhausting to teach in Spanish all day. Further, my aides were more linguistically competent than I, in spite of all my professional qualifications. (Meade-Roberts, 1988)

And so Jane called Betty Jones, who had been her graduate advisor at Pacific Oaks, to say, "I'll take you out to breakfast at the CAEYC conference. I need someone to talk to." That March breakfast led to Betty's making an April consulting visit to Soledad, the beginning of her seven-year connection with San Vicente.

The preschool had morning and afternoon sessions and was team-taught by Jane and a former Head Start teacher, with two aides. All but Jane were native Spanish speakers. Because of her involvement in other Title VII activities, Jane was often out of the classroom, and she was worried that her teammates might be resentful. However, in conversation with Betty as facilitator, they made it clear that this was the best job they'd ever had, they were feeling competent, and Jane could come and go as she pleased. That proved empowering to everyone, with Jane needing to let go of some of the being-in-charge she had assumed as the only credentialed teacher on the team, and others asserting their competence as full team members, not assistants.

Telling our stories: Staff development and classroom visiting

Taking leadership in staff development planning was part of Jane's job description. Before the Title VII project began, staff development was planned districtwide. During the first year of the project, Jane, Joan, and the project director initiated site planning, which led to a new style of in-service: a minimum day at San Vicente during which staff had choices among a variety of workshops led by their colleagues, teachers at the school who volunteered to share something that they believed they did well. The choice model was deliberate: If teachers have never had the experience of making choices for themselves, they are unlikely to permit children to make choices; and choice making is an important part of developmentally appropriate curriculum in early childhood.

In the second year San Vicente had its own staff development plan with a series of 17 in-house offerings, most led by teachers and scheduled for 50 minutes after school. Teachers were expected to choose eight sessions to attend. In addition, a minimum day provided two sessions with outside consultants—one on motor development, the other on whole language activities. Betty returned to lead the whole language session, which was set up as several learning centers from which teachers could choose. Teachers varied in their responsiveness; but one, Anne Solomon, still remembered her experience in a conversation two years later:

> That was a real aha! for me. I started a couple of activities that didn't interest me, and so I left them and moved on, still looking. Then I got to the incomplete sentences, and I got so excited that I stayed for the rest of the afternoon and wrote and wrote. I realized that if that's how I learn, kids must learn that way too.

Betty also made herself available to visit classrooms—to get acquainted, to observe, and to do something with children if invited. She was welcomed by some of the teachers.

Both the revised in-service plan and Betty's classroom visits introduced storytelling as a staff-development strategy. Teachers sharing their experiences select, organize, and tell their stories to other teachers, who share stories of their own, reaffirming that they are people with good ideas. Betty shared her observations in informal conversations with teachers and sometimes in writing. Doing activities with children, she wasn't necessarily viewed by teachers as a model, simply as another experience for the children—a new classroom "story" that teachers could observe, critique, and borrow ideas from if they chose.

Betty also wrote brief reports to the principal and to the superintendent after each visit, focusing on examples of creativity and growth. Her stories eventually found their way into the Title VII Program Evaluation, which she was hired to prepare, and into several publications (see For fur-

---

"We're Doing Something Interesting and Important Here"

Developmentally appropriate practice in early childhood education—which acknowledges children as active, interactive learners—can serve as a fine framework for planning staff development to empower teachers as active, interactive learners. Such staff development is characterized by

1. choice among alternatives;

2. peer interaction: "This is what's happening in my classroom. What's happening in yours?"; and

3. storytelling

- by teachers about children,
- by facilitators about children and teachers, and
- by everyone to new audiences—visitors to the school or other teachers attending conferences and workshops.

ther information, p. 87). Betty, Joan, Jane, and several teachers also presented at conferences, sharing our experience with a wider audience; and visitors from other districts observed at the school. We're doing something interesting and important here, was the message conveyed through all of these retellings.

Elisabeth Nichols

Grade-level meetings: Teachers work together

Tasks delegated to teachers are frequently accomplished through grade-level meetings. Meetings having to do with textbook selection and child placement continued as they always had. Under Title VII a new task was added: creation of a readiness checklist, which evolved into a developmental profile.

This task was slow to get under way. In the second year of the project, Joan met with first grade teachers to ask, "What do you look for in assessing a child's growth? How do you know if a child is ready for first grade?" Teachers were asked to follow up by making written lists, which some did. Many of the items generated by this process reflected the screening tests and the reading and math frameworks with which the teachers were familiar, and they were stated in deficit terms ("The child can't...").

In the third year Joan turned the lists over to Jane, who enlisted Betty's help. Increased district emphasis on outcomes made it possible for us to reconceptualize the task as developmental assessment of children's strengths, not deficits. We were committed to these principles:

1. Growth takes place in a developmental sequence, in which each stage is important.

2. Different children grow at different rates, and age norms to be met by all children in a group are inappropriate.

3. Each child grows at different rates in different areas of development.

4. It is important to make Piaget's distinction between social knowledge—what teachers teach directly—and logical knowledge—what children construct for themselves through action and interaction.

5. Learning is motivated by assessment that fosters self-esteem in both children and parents.

Kindergarten

Talking with kindergarten teachers, we asked, "What can your capable children do? What can the less capable children do?" Taking these ideas and the first grade teachers' lists, we combined the curriculum areas identified by teachers with the developmental categories we carry in our heads and came up with (1) literacy skills, (2) numeracy skills, (3) physical development, and (4) social skills. We decided that teachers' many social-knowledge items and expectations for acceptable

Soledad kindergartens, as is typical in California schools, have morning and afternoon sessions taught by different teachers. The morning teacher assists during part of the afternoon session and vice versa. Teachers were thus able to fill in for their partners during a meeting for all of the morning or all of the afternoon teachers.

behavior could be subsumed under category (5), ability to meet school/teacher expectations. We decided that curiosity and creativity were high on *our* list of goals for children's growth and added them as (6). Then we identified subcategories for each category and sequenced behaviors in each. What we were preparing was a draft for teachers to react to and change.

We tried out our draft on Joan, who gave us the go-ahead. Then back we went to the teachers with the request that they try rating half-a-dozen children (their highest and lowest achievers) on the profile to see what worked for them and what didn't. This experience set the stage for a half-day meeting, during a meal at a local hotel, at which we invited teachers to tell us everything they didn't like about the profile. We began, in fact, with a *complaints* checklist and tallied its results to serve as a take-off point for discussion.

Specific suggestions were made, questions were asked, and disagreements were voiced. The major concern expressed was, "I don't *know* some of those things about my children." ("I don't even know what some of those things [notably conservation] *are*.") Since introducing developmental theory to teachers was in fact part of our agenda in designing the profile, we

discussed conservation of number at some length at this point in the meeting.

In some of the kindergarten classrooms, teachers made clear, there was no opportunity for children to practice writing spontaneously or to "work competently on notably complex, creative, imaginative, self-initiated tasks" (one of our definitions). All activities were teacher directed, and short time blocks did not allow for complex projects. Teachers' time was spent in leading groups, large and small, and overseeing children's moves from one activity to the next. They weren't free to observe children.

One teacher objected that even if she took time to observe children's social interaction, she couldn't assess their level of competence because they were speaking Spanish. "Could you ask your aide to observe for some of the profile items?" we asked. She guessed she could try. And two of the teachers, after extended discussion, decided that perhaps on Fridays they might replace their usual tight schedule with a long choice time, which would free children to be spontaneous and teachers to observe them in action.

Teachers questioned the logical ordering of some items on our continua; we agreed and made changes. Development of the

San Vicente is a bilingual school, and all teachers not certified bilingual were expected to study Spanish. Some teachers grew rapidly in their competence in using Spanish in their classrooms. Others, reluctant to risk making mistakes, continued to rely on native-speaking aides.

profile was an actively participatory process, although we retained our commitment to a developmental framework for assessing children's growth. Together we discovered our lack of knowledge in some areas (*Is* there a sequence in the development of motor skills by four- and five-year-olds? We didn't know). We were especially delighted when a teacher who had used the profile for a while said, "You know what? Social knowledge doesn't scale. There's no logical order to learning shapes and colors and letters and your address." We had learned that by studying Piaget; we admired her for discovering it for herself.

During the fourth year kindergarten teachers again had two half-days at the hotel to review the profile now in use as the report card. Their increasing enthusiasm and increasing questions about the rationale for profile items led Joan to request, and the superintendent to approve, a full-day kindergarten in-service held away from school at a community center in a nearby town. Betty and Jane facilitated the in-service, focusing on developmental theory, which the teachers had said they wanted to know more about if they were going to implement a developmental program. All of the teachers also had planned time to share ideas of their own with the group.

First grade

Upon becoming principal at San Vicente, Joan began to make some changes in the kindergarten staff, and by the third year more than half of the eight teachers were persons she had hired. Furthermore, nearly all were able and willing to use Spanish in the classroom with increasing fluency. In half of the classrooms, Spanish and English alternated daily as the language of instruction at group time. In contrast, most of the first grade teachers were the veterans of the school who had

been on staff in prebilingual days. They were, with a couple of exceptions, unenthusiastic about change and especially about Spanish. They saw their own long-term commitment as evidence of greater devotion to the children than was the language fluency of persons hired just because they spoke Spanish. Comments to this effect were made in the teachers' room and in casual conversation. These feelings came out into the open when, in the fourth year, the first grade teachers met after school with the task of extending the kindergarten profile into a first grade profile.

Betty and Jane had had one meeting with first grade teachers the previous year. At that time we took the kindergarten profile as we had developed it and omitted the first two items on the left side of each continuum, leaving room to add two more on the right. At the meeting we divided the profile categories among task groups of two or three teachers and asked each group to write their results on a large sheet of paper. Teachers participated effectively but without great enthusiasm.

Marilyn Nolt

By the next year first grade teachers were coping unwillingly with a change in the structure of primary language-arts instruction. Because Soledad was newly implementing bilingual education, the Title VII grant had been written to provide funding for three bilingual support teachers (BSTs). It never proved possible, however, to find enough teachers qualified to teach Spanish reading who were willing to do so in a push-in program. The job was less appealing than regular classroom teaching, to which BSTs returned as soon as they could. As one explained, "You teach practically the same lesson eight times a day for 20 minutes. It's too structured. There's not enough choice for children or for the teacher; and that's all the Spanish most children get during the day."

A new plan for language-arts instruction in first and second grades was therefore devised. With seven classrooms at each grade level, teachers in three classrooms took Spanish-reading children from their own and other classes while their English-reading children moved to other classes for one and a half hours each morning. In several classrooms Spanish was also used at other times during the day. In first grade, however, the plan was complicated by the fact that only two teachers were fluent in Spanish. The third teacher responsible for Spanish reading was a reluctant conscript, assisted by a BST

aide and another aide borrowed from the other teachers.

It was in this context that we tried to have a meeting to complete the first grade profile. Sparked by their colleague's extreme discontent in her unsought role as Spanish language-arts teacher, and taking advantage of Joan's presence at the meeting, teachers protested their inability to use the profile with their children. "We are too fragmented. We don't know our children well enough to rate them" because of all the teaming. "Why can't we go back to having BSTs?" (The two Spanish-reading teachers who felt competent in this role had less to say; in fact, they had experienced the BST plan as inadequate and saw the team plan as more effective in meeting children's needs for Spanish literacy instruction.)

The teachers' anger led to a change of agenda, concentrating on the venting of complaints. The whole idea of the profile was questioned: "It's contradictory to the report card, and are we going to have to use both?" There was no unanimity about which they preferred. Finally someone said, "Well, if you're going to make us do this developmental stuff, the least you could do is in-service us in it." The meeting broke up with no progress on the profile.

Betty called Joan that evening with the intent of sympathizing, expecting her to have felt attacked, and instead found her delighted to have a teacher request for in-service, which she could use in asking the superintendent for teacher release time. He had already approved a day's in-service for kindergarten teachers; and faced with the teachers' request, he approved provision of substitutes to enable all first grade teachers to spend all day at the local hotel with Doris Smith, a member of the State Readiness Task Force, explaining its recommendations; several of the teachers sharing their knowledge of whole language strategies; and Betty facilitating discussion of teaming and program planning in first grade. It was, on the whole, a cheerful meeting. At the end Joan said, "Thank you for your participation. And I expect to see some evidence of whole language in your classrooms next year."

There was, as it turned out, considerable exploration of whole language strategies in the first grades following this meeting, and work on the profile resumed, as well, in the next year. First and then second grade teachers agreed on a revised profile for language arts. The same profile applies in both first and second grade, the second grade teachers decided; we don't need to add anything more. Those teachers who were trying a more developmental approach became increasingly dissatisfied with the existing report card; it no longer reflected what they were doing. "Weren't we going to use the profile for a report card?" they asked.

They no longer had a responsive principal ready to support them in this next step, however. Joan had moved into a district curriculum position, and the new principal was unready to consider making changes of any kind.

Sources of conflict

Conflict is an inevitable ingredient in the process of change. It may be useful rather than destructive if it can be used as a source of energy toward constructive change. A major turning point in this partnership took place when the first grade teachers' frustration got openly expressed and the principal, instead of feeling threatened by their anger, saw it as an opportunity to provide them with one of the things they requested—in-

---

Conflict as a Source of Energy for Change

1. Teachers often resist change.

2. Administrators often try to avoid conflict, regarding outward harmony as evidence of a good school.

3. Unexpressed conflicts within a school often lead to backbiting, passive-aggressive behavior, and apathy.

4. Appropriately expressed conflict gets real differences out in the open and releases energy that can be channeled into collaborative problem solving.

5. An external facilitator identified with neither side can sometimes be useful as observer/mediator.

6. Administrators who become too anxious when conflict surfaces are well advised not to initiate change.

---

service to help them become more competent in what they were being asked to do. She had, in fact, provoked their outburst in the first place by her calculated assignment of a reluctant teacher to Spanish language arts. That teacher agreed to a transfer to Gabilan School for the following year, provided she wouldn't have to teach Spanish. Her move freed a position for a new first grade teacher who was able and willing to teach Spanish; the other first grade teachers, freed from defending her out of loyalty, found themselves enjoying the challenge of change making in their classrooms.

Any external facilitator perceived by teachers as trustworthy will hear a good many of their complaints about the system, the principal, the parents, and working conditions in general. She can decide whether to remain noncommittal, sympathize, pass the word along, or encourage teachers to action. The latter course risks her relationship with administration; trust building and maintenance is a continuing challenge in both directions.

In this partnership our three-way relationship was fostered by real and growing respect for each other's competence in the context of a shared philosophy about early childhood education. We didn't agree about everything; for example, Joan was trained in Gesell testing and instituted developmental screening for all entering children. She introduced a preschool that, in effect, built in an extra year of school for some five-year-olds, and later added a two-year kindergarten that did the same, in response to high retention rates in kindergarten. Betty, with a theoretical bias against retention, was challenged to look thoughtfully at Joan's reasoning, within the social/political climate of the school and community and also with the added variable of second-language learning. Betty found herself wondering, Is it unreasonable that chil-

dren who are becoming fluent in two languages might need an extra year of school? Her colleague Doris Smith, coming to share an in-service and bringing recent experience as a member of the state readiness task force that recommended firmly against retention or delayed school entry, offered challenge from the other side of the issue. It was a good place in which to keep learning.

As principal, Joan practiced the fine art of getting along with a superintendent until he kicked her upstairs into a district curriculum position. Her successor as principal, appointed from within the school, had neither the negotiating skills nor the background in early childhood education to enable her to sustain leadership in the profile-development process. Instead, she put up roadblocks, expressing her anxiety that the profile might not be congruent with district objectives. The first grade teachers took initiative; they asked the consultant to come back, this time to discuss strategy, and talked about going over the principal's head to the superintendent. Another year passed; another principal, and then still another, came to San Vicente. The profile was not yet the primary report card, but teaching had changed in many classrooms.

Empowering teachers

Empowering teachers was an intended outcome of this project. This represents a radical change in those public school settings where teachers are accustomed to do whatever is mandated while complaining about it and the children, or to keep their doors shut and do their own thing. We saw empowerment in teachers' speaking out to administrators, considering their potential influence on main-office decisions, requesting in-services and consultation, and taking increasing responsibility for leadership among themselves. We saw empowerment in changes made in classrooms as teachers were challenged to explore changes consistent with their individual styles while being more responsive to children's individuality. We saw empowerment in teachers' sharing ideas with peers at in-services, welcoming to their classrooms visitors from other school districts who had heard about the project, and, in several cases, making presentations at professional conferences, encouraged by and sometimes teamed with Jane and Joan.

Anne Solomon, the kindergarten teacher who was an early enthusiast about the project, kept learning Spanish and growing in confidence, and she ended up teaming with Jane in the Spanish-immersion preschool. When Anne married and moved away, she took her experience at San Vicente to another school district, where she has taken an active leadership role while teaching kindergarten. She has organized in-services (Betty came for one), worked with staff to develop their own kindergarten developmental profile, and disseminated her learning through conference presentations. When Betty got a consulting request from still another school district, whose teachers had heard Anne talk and who were developing *their* own profile, it was clear that these ideas were moving into wider and wider circles through teacher leadership.

What was taught, what was learned, and what are the implications?

Over a five-year period it proved possible, given the resources provided by a project grant, to institute significant changes in a public primary school, both in teacher–child interactions and in teachers' initiative in working with each other. Among the things we learned are these:

• Public school teachers can move toward more developmentally appropriate practice if they are given good reasons for doing so and are directly involved in network building and in-service planning and implementation.

• A combination of administrative "fixing" and external facilitation can be particularly effective in initiating and sustaining change.

• Trust building takes time; teachers are justifiably skeptical of the quick fix. It is important that supportive relationships be sustained over several years.

• Classroom visiting and informal storytelling are useful strategies in both trust building and encouraging self-reflection by teachers.

• Conflict is inevitable when teachers believe that their competence or values are threatened. If their concerns are taken seriously, the energy generated by anger is an effective motivator for change.

• Personnel changes resulting from district politics or inevitable staff attrition may permanently interrupt a change process or, conversely, demonstrate the extent to which teachers have made it their own.

For further information

Jones, E., & Meade-Roberts, J. (1990). *Assessment through observation: A profile of developmental outcomes.* Occasional paper. Pasadena, CA: Pacific Oaks College. 14 pp. $1.75. (Includes the profile as report card)

Jones, E., & Meade-Roberts, J. (1991). Assessment through observation: A profile of developmental outcomes (ages 5–8). In L.Y. Overby (Ed.), *Early childhood creative arts: Proceedings of the International Early Childhood Creative Arts Conference* (pp. 44–50). Washington, DC: National Dance Association. (Available through NAEYC)

Parker-Whitney School report card (Rocklin District, California). Contact Anne Solomon, 6627 Derby Ct., Citrus Heights, CA 95621.

Other suggested readings

Agee, J.L. (1988). *Here they come: ready or not. Report of the School Readiness Task Force.* Sacramento, CA: California Department of Education.

Almy, M., & Genishi, C. (1979). *Ways of studying children.* New York: Teachers College Press.

Bredekamp, S. (Ed.). (1987). *Developmentally appropriate practice in early childhood programs serving children from birth through age 8.* Washington, DC: NAEYC.

Carini, P.F. (1975). *Observation and description: An alternative methodology for the investigation of human phenomena.* Grand Forks: North Dakota Study Group on Evaluation, University of North Dakota.

Cummins, J. (1986). Empowering minority students: A framework for intervention. *Harvard Educational Review, 56*(1), 18–36.

Cummins, J. (1989). *Empowering minority students.* Sacramento: California Association for Bilingual Education.

Genishi, C. (Ed.). (1992). *Ways of assessing children and curriculum: Stories of early childhood practice.* New York: Teachers College Press.

Kamii, C. (Ed.). (1990). *Achievement testing in the early grades: The games grown-ups play.* Washington, DC: NAEYC.

National Association for the Education of Young Children. (1988). NAEYC position statement on standardized testing of young children 3 through 8 years of age. *Young Children, 43*(3), 42–47.

Van Hoorn, J., Nourot, P., Scales, B., & Alward, K. (1993). *Play at the center of the curriculum.* New York: Merrill/Macmillan.

Reference

Meade-Roberts, J. (1988). It's *all* academic! In E. Jones (Ed.), *Reading, writing and talking with four, five and six year olds.* Pasadena, CA: Pacific Oaks College.

To contact the authors, write

Joan Hillard, Superintendent, Spreckels Union School District, P.O. Box 7308, Spreckels, CA 93962.

Elizabeth Jones, Pacific Oaks College, 5 Westmoreland Place, Pasadena, CA 91103.

Jane Meade-Roberts, 815 Capistrano Drive, Salinas, CA 93901.

Subjects & Predicates

I n all of the programs previously described, the partnership was established with an agency that expected its employees to benefit from the partnership. In the next three partnerships, facilitators worked with teachers volunteering from different programs rather than with a program as a whole. Individual initiative defined participation. Predictably, a somewhat different population was served.

Unlike the other partnerships described in this collection, which are products of the 1980s and 1990s, Mountain View Center was a 1970s creation. In its 12-year history it had widespread impact on the development of preschool and integrated elementary curriculum, which has again become timely in the 1990s as developmentally appropriate practice gains credibility in public school early childhood programs.

Everyone involved in Mountain View's advisory work with teachers in the Boulder Valley and Denver schools had significant autonomy. Schools as organizations were not the focus; the work was with self-selected teachers whose motivation was their curiosity and desire for growth.

The partnership was initiated, not by school personnel, but by a university faculty member. Like several of the other partnerships, it was defined not only as community service but also as collaborative research: What can project staff learn from, about, and with teachers by working closely with them? and how can we disseminate what we learn to the larger educational community?

Chapter 6

Co-Creating Primary Curriculum: Boulder Valley Schools

Maja Apelman

<hr>

Notes From the Storyteller*

<hr>

Celia took her first trip to the brick factory the year before we started to work together. She had heard that it was "a neat place to go" and visited it with her first graders. Dating back to the early years of the community, the factory is a local plant where you can observe the entire process of brick manufacture, from the crushing, mixing, and sifting of the dry clay to the loading of stacks of fired bricks onto trucks that go to building sites all over Colorado and neighboring states.

I met Celia in the 1975 Mountain View Center summer workshop. Celia was teaching in a Follow Through program that placed great emphasis on social studies—a subject that she did not feel comfortable

Here the storyteller is Maja Apelman, describing several years of going to the brick factory with Celia, a first grade teacher, in her work as a teachers' center advisor.

teaching. I invited her to attend a series of discussions on developing curriculum in social studies that I led during the workshop. She came to all of the sessions and at the end of the workshop asked me if I could continue to work with her.

I was happy to do so, and we arranged to meet in August to make plans for a social studies curriculum for the fall semester. It revolved around the children themselves, their families, their homes, and their parents' work.

In the spring of 1976, Celia wanted to return to the brick factory. The previous year she had taken the children there with almost no preparation. This year the children had taken walks through the neighborhood, looking at building materials. They saw many houses made of different-colored bricks and started to ask questions about where bricks came from, how the different colors were made, and so on. They also knew that the father of one of the children in class was a truck driver at the brick factory, and they were excited at the prospect of seeing bricks made.

I encouraged Celia to ask for two guides at the factory so that the children could be taken through all of the different areas in two separate groups. The trip was tiring but exciting for both the children and the accompanying adults. Follow-up activities went on for several weeks—writing, drawing and painting, block building, as well as work with clay collected at the site. We were surprised at how much the children remembered and how involved they were with their work.

The following fall one of the parents invited the new first graders to her dairy farm, and after the trip Celia and I had a brainstorming session on possible related activities. A week or so later, however, Celia told me that she didn't want to do the farm. "It's not my thing. It's important for me to be excited about what I'm doing." We tossed around some building-related ideas, but again Celia backed away from that topic. "I *really* want to do the brick factory again," she told me, "but I want to start earlier this year so that we have lots of time for follow-up."

And so we went to the brick factory in November, this time accompanied by a former teacher who was an expert photographer. After our trip she gave Celia and the children a beautiful book recording both the trip and the children's posttrip classroom activities.

In the spring Celia wanted to return to the brick factory, although she wondered if she could take the same children. I suggested that we divide the class into smaller groups, each one going to a different place. A lot of preparation was needed for this trip. Celia, her teaching assistant, an interested parent, a preschool teacher friend, and I all went to the factory to see which areas we should focus on and who would be in charge of each chosen area. Would there be enough to see for each group? Celia worried. Would the children want to go to more than their special area?

After extensive preparations we started out on a beautiful day in early May. Every group spent more time than anticipated, and every leader reported that they could have spent even more time in their area! On the way back Celia confessed, "I had this dream that nobody would focus and that all the kids were just jumping all over in their groups and I kept saying over and over, 'Look at the conveyer belts!'"

The following year Celia wanted to return to the brick factory, but this time she thought that everyone should first go to the clay mountain. The small group that went there on our last trip had a great time digging the dry clay. Celia wanted this experience for the whole class.

To prepare for this trip, she set up an area in her room where children could experiment with various raw materials she provided. She also asked all of the children to bring a sample of their own backyard "dirt." There were magnifiers, sieves, and plastic tubes to see how long it took water to seep through the various soils.

On a rather chilly November day, we set off, loaded with buckets, trowels, magnifiers, and water—to be able to mix with the clay on site. Again Celia worried that there might not be enough to do on the clay mountain, and again the children showed us how involved they can get if they are properly prepared and accompanied by interested and supportive adults.

In February Celia took the class to the brick factory, touring the establishment in two separate groups. I went along as photographer, taking pictures of the work done by men and machines. I wanted Celia to have a record of all of the processes so she could use the pictures for a book for the children.

After the trip Celia had a discussion with the children during which she drew a picture-map of the plant's layout—a suggestion I had made the previous year. I had thought of making such a map ahead of time and then going over it with the children, but Celia improved on my suggestion: she made the map *with* the children. "We're going to make a map of how the brick company is laid out," she told them, "so I want you to think in your mind what we saw first. What would we put right here?"

As the children remembered, Celia drew pictures on the map. Encouraged by her the children recalled each step. "Now, what was happening here? Who remembers?...Then what comes next? What was down here?...Where do the conveyer belts go to?...What was in that building? Who remembers?" When the whole layout was reconstructed, with input from the children, Celia went back to the beginning. This time, however, she asked the children to describe what they had seen. "Who can describe the dinosaur machine? What did it look like?...Who can make the sound the air bags made?...Who touched the bricks after they came out of the kiln? What did they feel like?" It was a great way to reconstruct the trip with the children.

My work with Celia was now quite different from what it had been when we began working together several years earlier. She no longer needed my help for organizing trips or follow-up activities, but she still wanted to have talks with me about curriculum and about individual children.

In April Celia was ready to return to the brick factory one more time. She asked me if I could come along and take one of the small groups. Because I was not spending much time in Celia's classroom at this point, I encouraged her to tape all of the children's discussions that preceded and followed the trip. I wanted to document this last trip through these discussions,

hoping that they would provide a record of the children's learning.

When Celia told the children about the return trip, she first described how they would be going in small groups. She listed the different areas and then simply said,

I'd like to discuss now what you would like to find out on this trip to the brick company. Think about our last trip when we had a whole tour of the entire brick company. Is there a specific thing that you would like to find out that you didn't get to find out on the last trip? And you can also be thinking of the group you'll choose to go on.

It was two-and-a-half months since the last trip. Here are examples of the children's questions and comments:

I want to find out how the conveyer belts run, if they have a motor...how they put the bands around the bricks.... I want to know how they put the fire in the kiln.... I want to ask why they put five holes in some bricks.... I was going to find out how they fill those bags with air in the dinosaur so the bricks won't fall out.

When children asked questions that weren't to the point, Celia reminded them of the purpose of the return trip. "Think about your last trip and about something you saw that you didn't quite understand. That's what we're going back to find out."

Larissa: How do they put different colors in one brick?

Susan: They told us that.

Celia: Well, Larissa wants to find out. She didn't quite understand it.

Celia valued every child's question and supported the desire to learn. Sometimes other children came up with the answers:

Michael: How do they get those little specks in the bricks?

Jean: I know that. The man said they grind the stuff that's not very good and put it in new bricks.

Carl: I know about the yellow specks. See, the guy said that they put in something special to take out all the oxygen and that changes the color too.

Celia: Well, let's check it out. Maybe all those things happen.

Clearly these children were keen observers, had remembered many details, and easily accepted their teacher's reason for going back to learn more. Not understanding something, asking questions, expecting to learn from their own observations as well as from the knowledge of interested adults—all of this was taken for granted by these first graders. It is clear that children are capable of much concentration and understanding when a situation supports learning.

It was hard for me to think back to the days when I started my work with Celia—when she told me that she hated trips and was "terrified" of discussions. Now she was able to explain why:

> I didn't really know how to ask questions and how to get children to talk. Now I just start and the kids talk back and forth and they're really good. I'm always thinking about what they want to find out, what they want to know. I don't even know if I thought that was important before. So many teachers don't really give kids credit for being able to think. What are teachers worrying about? The kids have got the questions. Just ask them.

The setting and the people

My work with Celia and other public school primary teachers took place when I was a teacher-advisor on the staff of Mountain View Center for Environmental Education in Boulder, Colorado. (The overall goal of the center was defined as "education through fuller use of all the environments in which children live— physical, social, natural—and the environments of books, ideas, and history.") Funded by the Ford Foundation, the state of Colorado, and the National Science Foundation, and located on the campus of the University of Colorado from 1970 to 1982, the center was directed by David and Frances Hawkins and was modeled after an advisory center in Leicestershire, England. David was a professor of philosophy at the university, with special interests in the philosophy of science and of education. Frances, a former preschool and kindergarten teacher, had great expertise in early childhood education. They created a very special learning atmosphere.

Our staff of eight included two types of advisors: generalist advisors like me, who had considerable classroom experience and who drew primarily on that experience in their work with teachers (although they also had special strengths and interests in subject-matter areas, such as reading and social studies), and specialist advisors, whose contributions were primarily in their subject-matter knowledge. We had experts in science—especially physics and botany—mathematics, arts and crafts, and music. Some specialists had extensive teaching experience and familiarity with classrooms, while others' classroom experience was limited. Most of their work was at the center, teaching workshops and being available to teachers for consultation, but they also went into classrooms, alone or with one of the generalist advisors. Their success with teachers and children grew out of their enthusiasm for their subject matter and their desire to share this knowledge. It was important for teachers to see how children responded to new subject matter and to a different style of teaching. Even though teachers generally cannot devote themselves fully to just a few children at a time, seeing the work that the children produced and the thinking that they were capable of under these circumstances often changed teachers' expectations, and their classroom activities became richer and more diverse.

All of the advisors offered seminars and workshops for preschool and elementary teachers. Classes met weekly for 8 to 10 sessions—after school, in the early evening, and occasionally on Saturdays. The classes were free unless teachers chose to earn university credit, and they were limited to about 12 participants. In addition we ran an intensive two-week summer institute with an enrollment of 20 to 30 people.

The emphasis in all of the courses was on teachers' own learning. Exploring materials in science and mathematics, becoming familiar and comfortable with growing plants, learning to weave or make baskets, using an assortment of musical instruments—many of them homemade— playing language games, exploring the community and using its resources—all of this was taught at an adult level to interest the teachers themselves. Teachers could borrow materials to try out in their classrooms, and they were encouraged and helped to make materials in our woodworking shop.

Defining ourselves as teacher-advisors, Mountain View staff believed in

1. providing assistance only upon the request of the teacher;

2. having no evaluative or supervisory function;

3. having no predetermined agenda and not imposing or implementing mandated programs;

4. providing assistance in terms of teachers' needs, goals, and objectives;

5. acting as a support and resource person for the professional growth of teachers and helping them develop more effective educational programs for children;

6. respecting teachers' autonomy and working toward strengthening teachers' independence; and

7. developing long-term collegial relationships based on mutual trust and respect.

But is it relevant?

The funding that was available to support teachers' centers such as Mountain View in the 1970s is, for the most part, no longer with us. There are, however, teachers' centers in a number of places, a few of them surviving from the 1970s. They may be sponsored by resource-and-referral agencies, children's museums, Head Start programs, school districts, or a consortium of community

Teachers' centers have been described as "places and programs for staff development that are designed and used by teachers on their own volition to fill their self-identified training and curriculum needs" (Buxton, 1972, p.1). Teachers' centers operate from the assumption that teachers have the most accurate information for assessing their professional needs, based on direct individual experience in their classrooms, schools, and community. A teachers' center is "*developmental* in its view of how teachers learn; *integrated* and *substantive* in its choice of curriculum; and *supportive*, *active*, *nonevaluative* and *professional* in its style of working with teachers" (p. 7).

During the 1970s national interest in open education and integrated curriculum, influenced by the innovation taking place in some British primary schools, led to the creation of many resource centers for preschool and elementary teachers. These centers drew on the progressive tradition initiated many decades earlier in this country by John Dewey and others, as well as on early childhood education principles and on growing concern for math, science, and environmental education. Suggestions for further reading on this history are given at the end of this chapter.

Current trends in preschool and primary education toward developmentally appropriate practice, whole language, hands-on math and science, and critical thinking by both children and teachers are supported by this history of thought and practice. All of the stories in this book describe efforts to grow teachers in ways that are consistent with these trends, using early childhood education at its best as a model for teacher education.

agencies. Variously, they offer recycled materials; toy loan; dramatic-play kits; tools for making materials; published resources; and, sometimes, workshops for teachers and parents.

School district centers are often places to look for activity ideas, reproduce worksheets, and laminate things, rather than to engage in collaborative inquiry. In an era of tighter budgets, providing quality staff who are able to support inquiry by teachers is seen as too expensive. It is cheaper and more familiar to regress to the American tendency to rely on commercial materials, rather than relationship building, in support of teaching.

Mountain View offered both unusual, challenging materials and knowledgeable, enthusiastic staff. It was funded as both a demonstration and a research project; it sought to provide effective in-service support for teachers while studying teachers as learners. Its staff, in their advisory role, were scholars gathering data though collaboration with teachers. Each specialist had a room full of hands-on materials, enabling teachers to investigate selected

topics in math and physics, botany, and the arts and music, and to reflect on their growth in understanding. The expectation was that teachers would make the connection between their experience as learners

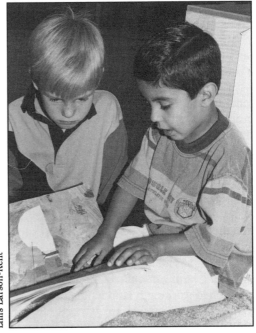

Lillis Larson-Kent

> Mountain View's exceptional resources enabled it to serve as a "think tank" for an inquiry approach to teaching and learning. This approach, which emphasizes teaching as a craft, has a long tradition grounded in the theories of John Dewey, who saw education as a democratic process of collective inquiry, and Jean Piaget, who emphasized the importance of learners' constructing their own knowledge.

and children's experience as learners.

Staff modeled and shared their excitement about their areas of expertise, but they did not tell teachers how to teach. Some staff were more interested in how teachers think than in how teachers teach. They were thus able to ask genuine questions of teachers who were exploring materials, rather than simply to give them information.

While my colleagues' interest was in teachers' construction of in-depth knowledge in the arts and sciences, I was more interested in how teachers construct their knowledge of *children.* I was also interested in the practical dilemmas faced by teachers in classrooms, as were the teachers themselves. All of us treated teachers as intellectuals—persons capable of sustained thought about interesting questions—and as professionals able to identify and pursue their own needs for growth.

Mountain View's relevance lies in its documentation of principles of learning applicable to teachers as learners as well as to children and is based on deep respect for the learner. It emphasized *excellence,* a very current word in educational circles, although we never used the word. Under what conditions is it possible to achieve work of increasingly high quality by both teachers and children? These are goals for education everywhere.

Our work demonstrated the potential for involving highly qualified advisors in sustained working relationships with teachers, motivated by the opportunity for mutual learning. For the advisors, as for

the teachers, voluntary participation, continuity, and freedom from administrative pressures were important. As center staff members we were extraordinarily autonomous; each was free to pursue his or her own interests. We offered teachers comparable autonomy in their work with us. We didn't have conflicts with administrators in the schools because we didn't impose an agenda on teachers (I assured teachers that I wouldn't tell the principal what *they* were doing, although I might explain to her what goals *I* had for my work in their classes). Our work took place outside the usual constraints of the school system while contributing, in those schools whose administrators found the center's philosophy to some degree compatible, to outcomes desirable for that system.

Teacher development strategies

Advisors in *any* setting can begin working with teachers from many starting points. A teacher may request help in a particular subject area, regarding problems with a particular child or group of children, or with matters of organization and scheduling. Some teachers feel more comfortable if they start with a conference; others may ask for a general classroom observation with subsequent feedback. Even if teachers do not have a specific request, they usually have a general idea of the direction in which they wish to move. The success of advisory work depends on a relationship of mutual trust and respect, which develops gradually as teacher and advisor work and learn together through their attempts to solve the problems of daily teaching.

I spent at least half of my time in classrooms—observing, assisting, and interacting with children. My work developed from teachers' stated needs and included helping with management problems; observing individual children; leading discussions so that teachers could see the involvement of children if they were interested in a subject; changing room arrangements to create better learning environments; introducing new materials and activities; assisting with trip planning and curriculum development; and encouraging greater use of community resources.

When teachers asked me to observe in their classrooms, I first asked for permission to take notes, explaining that I wished to write down things to be discussed after the observation. Later, when we sat down together, I put my open notebook on the table and used my remarks as starting points for our discussion. I always shared my classroom notes with teachers, although sometimes I made additional notes for myself later. I paid special attention to areas of teacher strengths because I always wanted to give some positive feedback. Later I used these strengths to move into areas of needed change.

Teachers often look at consultants with some degree of suspicion. They don't like outsiders to come in and tell them what to do. I found that my own classroom experience gave me credibility. Although many of the teachers I worked with told me that

they were quite nervous before my first visit, they soon relaxed and appreciated having an interested and supportive adult in their room. One teacher told me early in our work, "Never in all the years that I've been teaching has there been anyone in my room who didn't come to criticize. I don't mind you at all in my class; the kids could be all over and I wouldn't mind."

Sometimes I was surprised at teachers' reactions. I had worked with Joyce, a second grade teacher, over a period of two months. A road along the school playground was being paved, and we used this opportunity to observe and study all of the stages of road building. The children watched the work; took two related field trips—to a gravel mine and an asphalt plant; learned about the machinery, raw materials, and work processes; and did a lot of related classroom activities. At the end of this project, Joyce told me how much she valued my interest in the road paving. "You really got involved, and I felt it was sincere," she told me. Another teacher mentioned something similar: "I feel that we're sharing a lot of the learning together and a lot of the excitement of discovering new things. . . . I feel like you're really interested." I had never thought of my capacity to become "really interested" as anything special until teachers started mentioning it to me.

My classroom work was appreciated by the teachers, but lunchtime and after-school talks were just as important to them. In my early work with any teacher, I scheduled plenty of talking time. For teachers with whom I continued to work for several years, talking sessions were

When advisors treat teachers as capable thinkers, teachers keep thinking creatively about children, teaching, and the subject matter being taught. When teachers treat children as capable thinkers, children become increasingly interested in what is being studied, as Celia found in her study of the brick factory.

scheduled at their request. Face-to-face contact remained important for some teachers, but for others I sometimes wrote down my questions and suggestions. This might happen after a class trip or discussion or after a conversation with a teacher about developing a certain theme. I found that once I started to focus on a subject, I often got additional ideas. The first time I gave such notes to a teacher, she was so pleased that I began to do it more regularly. Teachers appreciated the fact that I continued to think about their classrooms after I left—just as they do—and although it was extra work initially, these notes were useful in the long run. They could be shared with other teachers, they provided a permanent reference for the teachers for whom they were written, and they gave me a written record of what I had suggested.

Giving feedback is an essential ingredient of advisory work. It helps to make connections for teachers and encourages them to become more reflective. After I had worked in Heather's room for several weeks, she told me, "I enjoy getting feedback. You don't often get it in educa-

tion. You're alone in your room. When the principal comes in, he isn't looking for the same things we are looking for."

Asked what was most helpful about my work with her, Sharon, a first grade teacher, answered,

> All the challenges she throws out and having her there observing, and just the immediate feedback on that from somebody who is kind of on the same wavelength. . . . After the kids leave, that's almost the most helpful time. We sit there and talk about it. She'll ask me questions and make comments about different things that happened and talk about different kids, just different problems. I sit there and write constantly the whole time I'm talking to her . . . probably the biggest help has been just kind of tying all these loose ends that I had together and making sense out of them. I've had reasons why I did everything, but none of them all tied together into a total program.

Later Sharon was asked to describe if and how her teaching had changed during the semester she worked with me:

> Instead of thinking about teaching something to my class, I spend a lot more time thinking about individual kids. . . . I feel like I've gotten to know each kid much better at this point in the year than I ever have before, and I feel like I'm teaching [the children] to learn things on their own. . . . I feel much more like a teacher.

Sharon was beginning to make connections. She was learning on her own, just as the children were.

Empowering teachers

Teaching is often lonely. There is no regular professional time built into most teachers' work week during which they can think and talk in-depth with other interested adults. Experienced teachers need opportunities to use their intellect—to have serious discussion about their work with each other and with advisors and ex-

© Robert Samuel

Teachers who think that they know all that there is to know about children and curriculum—who don't get excited by new insights into learning, by new approaches to subject matter, or by new ways of working with materials—will not serve their children well. Advisors continually challenge their advisees to become more thoughtful and reflective individuals who will remain learners for the rest of their lives. Teachers need to be learners, not only to experience the excitement and the satisfaction of gaining new insights and knowledge, but also because being engaged in their own learning will help them to understand and respect the many varied ways in which children learn—and that is critical for successful teaching. (Apelman, 1991, p. 77–78)

perts. Workshops and seminars at Mountain View offered teachers the opportunity to share common interests and problems.

One year, for instance, I worked with five first grade teachers who all felt a need for firmer grounding in child development. I organized biweekly sessions during which we would discuss problems that had come up in the different classrooms. After a few sessions I realized that these teachers lacked observation skills, so we concentrated on observing children in many different situations to begin to see patterns of behavior and learn how to diagnose problems.

In another year I decided to offer a weekly seminar that I called "Discussions about Teaching." Here is its description:

This is a course for teachers who have questions which they wish to discuss with colleagues: questions about their educational philosophy; questions about their curriculum as it relates (or does not relate) to the needs of children; questions about their teaching methods, about testing, and so on. One focus of the course will be on curriculum content: how to choose, develop, and organize appropriate subject matter for children of different ages, and how to extend and evaluate the learning that arises from it.

Since I am particularly interested in the problems faced by teachers who

want to put theory into practice, I hope to visit the schools of participating teachers and be available for individual conferences.

I thought that my work in schools would be strengthened if teachers could meet regularly with their colleagues, and I believed that knowing the classrooms and teaching styles of the participants first-hand would help me plan discussions of interest to all concerned. I also hoped that the teachers in this class would start an informal network so that like-minded individuals in the district could share experiences and get the support they often lacked. Teachers who have an interested audience of peers are encouraged to tell their stories, to think out loud, and to experience themselves as effective thinkers.

Mountain View's emphasis on adult learning was also intended to empower teachers as thinkers. We provided opportunities for teachers to learn at their own adult level, regardless of whether this learning would be of immediate use in the classroom. Too often teachers are expected to transmit knowledge that they have not sufficiently absorbed. When teachers experience the excitement that real learning generates, they transmit their enthusiasm about learning to the children they work with. At Mountain

View teachers were exposed to new knowledge and ideas, new ways of thinking, and new approaches to learning. Their efforts were respected, their questions taken seriously, and their learning and growth encouraged and supported.

What was taught, what was learned, and what are the implications?

Did we make a difference? Did we develop leaders? For more than a decade, Mountain View Center disseminated its experience nationally and internationally through publications and a steadily growing group of teachers attending summer institutes. Local teachers provided good attendance at our weekly open houses. Weekly seminars served a smaller group of teachers, some of whom invited us to work in their classrooms, as well.

As one of several advisors, I worked intensively with half-a-dozen teachers at a time and had additional shorter term contacts with a number of others. This aspect of our work can best be described as leadership development. We believed it worthwhile to invest in teachers who can be thought of as "growth points" in their schools—people with potential to influence others' growth. We made a point of referring teachers to others as resources; for example, I called on Celia several times to share her new trip-planning expertise with teachers from other schools. More formally, we received funding from the Teachers' Center Exchange to implement an Intern Advisor Program in the Boulder Valley School District. This grant paid substitutes to enable several teachers to take off one-half day a week to work in other teachers' classrooms, with supervision from Mountain View staff.

In our direct work with teachers and in our writing for publication, *we collected good stories to be retold*. Teaching and learning, we believed, can best be understood through many teachers' stories.

"Growth over time," David Hawkins has written, "is organic and uneven in character and notoriously does not respond to systemwide panaceas or 'models.'"

> In-depth work with teachers in their classrooms is a crucial part of the Center's program. It is here that the strengths and needs of each teacher can be taken into consideration. . . . in our work with teachers we are not rigid adherents of any narrowly defined "models" or "methods." Good teaching does have some universal characteristics but it also varies—as it should—from teacher to teacher and for different children in different areas of work. We learn from teachers' successes, and we claim no credit for these beyond our role as supporters, facilitators, and critics. This statement is an expression not of modesty but of a central philosophy about learning and teaching. The improvement of early education will not come about solely or even largely through the guiding efforts of any single group but through many kinds of professional support for all those engaged in it. (Mountain View Center brochure)

The advisory model, in which self-selected teachers are treated as serious collaborators in action-research on curriculum development, has been implemented in many teacher centers with a broader base than Mountain View and in a wide variety of advisory relationships. Its principles are clear. While it attracts relatively competent teachers, the advisory model recognizes that even the most competent teacher needs support when trying something new. It defines teachers as professionals who are able to identify and pursue their own needs for growth. Extended to other teacher populations, it may help to convince a broad range of less confident but competent practitioners that they are thinkers too.

For further information

Apelman, M. (1979). An advisor at work. In K. Devaney (Ed.), *Building a teachers' center* (pp. 157–168). San Francisco: Teachers' Center Exchange, Far West Laboratory for Educational Research and Development. (Distributed by Teachers College Press)

Apelman, M. (1981). *The role of the advisor in the inservice education of elementary school teachers: A case study.* Unpublished doctoral dissertation, University of Colorado, Boulder, CO.

Apelman, M. (1986). Working with teachers: The advisory approach. In K.K. Zumwalt (Ed.), *Improving teaching* (pp. 115–129). Alexandria, VA: Association for Supervision and Curriculum Development.

Apelman, M. (1991, Summer). Working with teachers. *Thought and Practice: The Journal of the Graduate School of Bank Street College of Education, 3*(1), 74–84.

Hawkins, D. (1974). *The informed vision: Essays on learning and human nature.* New York: Agathon.

Hawkins, F. (1986). *The logic of action.* Boulder: Colorado Universities Press.

Outlook magazine, published quarterly by Mountain View Center from 1971 to 1985. Boulder, Colorado.

Seckinger, B. (1978). *A look at the first year: Experienced teachers as advisors to their colleagues.* Unpublished master's project, Pacific Oaks College, Pasadena, CA.

Other suggested readings

Baker, W.E., Leitman, A., Page, F., Sharkey, A., & Suhd, M. (1971). The creative environment workshop. *Young Children, 26*(4), 219–223.

Bolin, F.S., & Falk, J. (Eds.). (1987). *Teacher renewal: Professional issues, personal choices.* New York: Teachers College Press.

Cruickshank, D.R. (1987). *Reflective teaching.* Reston, VA: Association of Teacher Educators.

Connelly, F.M., & Clandinin, D.J. (1988). *Teachers as curriculum planners: Narratives of experience.* New York: Teachers College Press.

Clift, R.T., Houston, N.R., & Pugach, M.C. (Eds.). (1990). *Encouraging reflective practice in education.* New York: Teachers College Press.

Devaney, K. (Ed.). (1979). *Building a teachers' center.* San Francisco: Teachers' Center Exchange, Far West Laboratory for Educational Research and Development. (Distributed by Teachers College Press)

Duckworth, E. (1987). *"The having of wonderful ideas" and other essays on teaching and learning.* New York: Teachers College Press.

Fosnot, C.T. (1989). *Enquiring teachers, enquiring learners: A constructivist approach for teaching.* New York: Teachers College Press.

Jervis, K., & Montag, C. (Eds.). (1991). *Progressive education for the 1990s: Transforming practice.* New York: Teachers College Press.

Kohl, H. (1984). *Growing minds: On becoming a teacher.* New York: Harper and Row.

Marshall, S. (1968). *Adventure in creative education.* New York: Pergamon.

Pathways: A Forum for Progressive Educators, and *Insights into Open Education.* Center for Teaching and Learning, Box 8158, University of North Dakota, Grand Forks, ND 58202. (Periodical collections of articles on teaching by classroom teachers and other educators)

Rogers, D.L., Waller, C.B., & Perrin, M.S. (1987). Learning more about what makes a good teacher good through collaborative research in the classroom. *Young Children, 42*(4), 34–39.

Weber, L. (1971). *The English infant school and informal education.* Englewood Cliffs, NJ: Prentice-Hall.

Yonemura, M. (1986). *A teacher at work: Professional development and the early childhood educator.* New York: Teachers College Press.

Reference

Buxton, A.P. (1979, June). A distinctive option in inservice: The teachers' center meets individual needs and institutional goals. Occasional Paper no. 5, Teachers' Center Exchange, Far West Laboratory for Educational Research and Development, San Francisco.

> **To contact the author, write**
> Maja Apelman, 755 Lincoln Place, Boulder, CO 80302.

I n the following chapter Barbara Creaser describes two similar partnerships under different auspices within Australian early childhood programs. As an advisor for the Kindergarten Union, Barb had direct access to teachers in their classrooms. Later, as a university faculty member, she observed in classrooms while supervising practicum students but did not have extended time to spend with teachers. Instead, she organized a monthly seminar for a small, invited group of teachers and challenged them to join her in collecting data on children's play. Like Maja at Mountain View, Barb worked with competent teachers who were interested in in-depth curriculum planning and comfortable in professional relationships.

These partnerships, in Adelaide and Darwin as in Boulder, involved teachers as co-investigators, using collaborative inquiry as the vehicle for teacher growth. Barb was initiating action research, selecting theories to share with teachers and asking, Does this work with the children you teach? The theories she selected focused on the importance of play in early childhood, and her question as teacher educator was, How can teachers be supported to value and articulate play as a mode of learning?

Chapter 7

Teachers as Observers of Play: Involving Teachers in Action Research

Barbara Creaser

_____ **Notes From the Storyteller*** _____

Not long after the four-year-olds made a trip to Yarrawonga Zoo, their teacher, Robyn, wrote these notes as she observed their play:

Tim: We trying to get the croc out.

Tom: Is he biting us?

Terry: Don't catch him, he's got big jaws.

Tim: We're trying to see how strong him are!

Tom: Can I help?

(Pause—moving between cages)

Clark: What's in there, mate?

Charlie: Birds.

Tom: I'm in his (the croc's) cage.

Tim: Get out, get out, he's going to bite!

Tom: No!

_____

Here the storytellers are Barb Creaser and several teachers with whom she collaborated on an investigation of play programming, sharing their observations of children at play.

Tim: Just 'tend.

Aaron: What are you doing?

Tom: We've got a torch [flashlight] for the crocodile.

Bert: (passing by) It looks like you're busy, guys.

Aaron: I've got a torch for me and a torch for the caterpillar. That's a parrot, not a possum.

Tom: You can pretend, can't you?

Aaron: You can pretend it to be a possum.

Bert: Hey look, the train's ready to go! Hey look, your train's ready to go!

Tim: Let's get our pillows.

Tom: Get two, get two.

Tim: Where do you want to go?

Tom: Do you want to go to the zoo?

Robyn's sharing of this observation was one of the many pieces of data we collected for discussion in our Play seminar. Our discussions enabled us to build generalizations. We found, for example, that there appears to be a recognizable, predictable sequence of events that lead to rich pretend play, among them,

• organizing to go on a trip to have a *real* experience;
• gathering the props that will help children adopt the roles associated with the play;
• setting up the scene with and without the children;
• joining in the play by taking on a relevant role; and
• asking some key questions of the players as you and they play.

"Children play the real experiences they have with their families in the community, too," Jo said. "Daniel asked me to be his patient last week, when he was Dr. Watson."

Jo: Hello, Daniel.

Daniel: I'm Dr. Watson. Can I listen to your heart?

Jo: Yes. Can you hear anything?

Daniel: No, not yet. You have chicken pox in your body. You can come with me to hospital. I'll give you some medicine. Here are your pills and water. Do you want a smoke?

Jo: No thanks.

Daniel: I think I better ring the nurse. . . . Hello, it's Dr. Watson. Yes, she's got chicken pox in her body. No, she doesn't smoke.

"Interesting," commented Judy. "I realize that I hardly ever see pretend smoking and drinking in the children's play. I wonder why not? They certainly see adults doing those things."

After further discussion Lyn asked, "Can I show you my videos of the twos' home scenes now?" And so we watched:

(Carly approaches Ella and Alice.)

Ella: Go away, Carly. We be sisters, Carly warly.

(Carly hovers nearby. Ella and Alice arrange the table and chairs and put plates, cups, and blocks on the table.)

Carly: Mum, can I play?

Ella: Owwah, you sit on my shirt. Cook, cook. I'm mummy aren't I? I like that.

Ella, to Alice: Could you have a drink for mummy?

Carly: A drink for baby.

Alice: You have to put the block in there (cup), and that's the ice.

Carly, to Alice: She said you're the mummy.

Ella: No, I'm the mummy.

Alice: No, I'm the mummy.

Ella: I am. You're very naughty. Look, look sister, baby's pulling your chair out.

Alice: She's crying, mummy.

(Pause)

Alice: The baby needs a bottle.

Ella: I got a bottle! I got a bottle!

(Alice goes to the cupboard to get a bottle but stops when she realizes that Ella is happy to feed the baby with an imaginary bottle.)

Alice (holding an imagined bottle to Ella): Here's a bottle.

Ella: I GOT A BOTTLE!

"Do the twos use the home corner the way you set it up?" asked Robyn.

"No," said Chris. "It doesn't seem to matter to some of my twos what I set up for dramatic play. They just go back to Mums and Babies and Sisters, and even if there's a nice home corner, they don't want to use it. When I invited them to, they said, 'No. We want to make our own.' And they did." Robyn agreed. She had had exactly the same experience with her fours wanting to create their own home.

"Children don't 'see' the environment in the same way we do," I suggested. "They see it in terms of dramatic play possibilities. A bed in the book corner becomes a boat. Do we move the bed or move the book corner? Can we be sufficiently flexible to allow the children some control over the environment?"

The setting

I have worked as a facilitator with teachers of young children in two Australian states in two different roles. In South Australia I was an advisor for the Kindergarten Union; in Northern Territory I was a university faculty member involving teachers in a research project. In both settings my interest was in encouraging teachers to support children's learning through play.

In Australia the three-year Diploma of Teaching in early childhood education certifies teachers of four- to eight-year-olds. Teachers in half-day kindergartens (for four-year-olds) earn public school salaries and teach morning and afternoon sessions. Some kindergartens are located on public school sites; others have their own buildings elsewhere in the community. Staff in full-day child care programs are certified by a two-year Associate Diploma and work on a lower pay scale. Most programs receive public subsidy.

South Australia: Preschoolers and print

The South Australian Kindergarten Union's 12 advisors, all experienced teachers, were responsible for the quality of environments and programs in the state's publicly subsidized kindergartens for four-year-olds. Within the Union's minimum standards, we were essentially autonomous in our work. Although we were expected to visit each center at least three times a year, we could choose to

work more intensively with some programs than with others, and teachers could invite us to do so if they chose. It was sometimes important to work intensively with one center if there were problems occurring. It was equally advantageous to visit some of the flourishing centers where advisors could become learners with the staff team by implementing new ideas. This was the context within which the Preschoolers and Print project was born.

When my fellow advisor Kay Parsons returned from graduate school at Wheelock College excited about literacy development in early childhood, we decided to invite a small group of teachers to become co-investigators with us. This study partnership was seen by the Kindergarten Union as an exciting new initiative that in the long run might improve the quality of many programs for children. Our advisor role gave us access to potentially interested teachers.

We sent a letter to six centers with which we were familiar, selecting them on the basis of three criteria: (1) the director was functioning well as a staff team leader, (2) the program was one that we believed was good for young children, and (3) it seemed likely that the staff would take on the extra work that the project involved with enthusiasm and energy. The staff, the parent group, and the management committee were all fully informed about what the project involved. All six centers decided to participate.

Six teachers and two advisors met in someone's home for about three hours monthly, from February through July. We read and discussed books on literacy

Working intensively with a small group of teachers as co-investigators, a facilitator is "growing" herself as well as the teachers. She becomes more knowledgeable in her continuing work with teachers, as they become more knowledgeable in their continuing work with children, parents, and peers.

> Experienced teachers can grow by collaborative investigation of new ideas that interest them. Through reading, data collection, experimentation in their own classrooms, and dialogue, mutual excitement is built. Comfortably scheduled meetings—one evening a month in someone's home—enabled this group of preschool teachers to sustain lively interest over half-a-year together.

development, and teachers enthusiastically experimented with the creation of print-rich environments in their classrooms. The ideas we read about made sense to all of us. They fit into our prior understanding of children's development, although they were discrepant with the belief most of us had entered early childhood education with—that reading and writing were the domain of compulsory schooling, and that preschool children's interest in these topics could be ignored. The readings supported our newer hunches about children, and there was an immediacy in what we were reading about, what we were trying out, and children's responses.

In our monthly discussions the teachers exchanged successes and failures. They arrived laden with examples of children's writing and with photographs of what had been taking place. By the time the meeting ended, the floor was usually covered with layers of papers. We found that children spontaneously practiced reading and writing if we gave them the resources necessary for practice and if we built the need for writing into the environment; for example, if there was a post office corner, there would be stamps, envelopes, writing paper, labels, forms, and pens and pencils. If a hospital was set up, there would be charts, prescriptions, and medical notes. The evidence of children's writing contradicted our past assumptions that preschoolers are too young for writing. For all of us this was genuine discovery, and teachers got positive feelings and feedback

about the opportunities they were creating for children. Some of the feedback came from parents, many of whom became at least as excited as the teachers over their child's reading and writing attempts.

This was an action research project, initiated by advisors out of their own curiosity and involving teachers as partners in investigation. When I moved to a university position in the Northern Territory, I took this experience with me. There I initiated another project focused on the topic I had, in the interim, explored in my graduate work at Pacific Oaks College—play.

Northern Territory: Play programming in early childhood settings

Northern Territory University in Darwin, where I joined the faculty following my experience with Preschoolers and Print, offers two teacher education strands: an Associate diploma for child care workers, and diploma and degree courses for teachers of four- to eight-year-olds. As a member of the Faculty of Education, I taught in both programs and thus had access to both schools and child care centers. This was the setting in which I undertook a new action research project, Play Programming in Early Childhood Settings.

The project was designed (1) to document self-directed sociodramatic play in a variety of early childhood settings (ages two through eight), (2) to encourage teachers to be self-critical and to change

Who are the people in an early childhood education community with the time, energy, and skills to facilitate teacher growth? Some of them hold designated advisory roles—advisor, consultant, trainer, educational coordinator, curriculum specialist. Some of them work at colleges and universities with ties to the community. Advisors are expected to improve the quality of teaching. College staff are often expected to conduct research. Both can meet *their* job expectations by collaborating with teachers-as-researchers.

their practice with regard to children's play, and (3) to discover unifying principles that underlie "play programming" across age settings in early childhood. Partners included the university's Faculty of Education, the Northern Territory Department of Education, four schools, and two child care centers.

The faculty has a research fund to which I applied for project support. This funding met the cost of relief staff for those participating teachers working in child care centers, as well as typing and production of the project report. Lyn Fasoli and I, both full-time faculty members, facilitated the group process and had access to university resources, including video cameras. The dean agreed to give credit for project participation to teachers who were enrolled in the Bachelor of Education program. One teacher was able to take advantage of this option, enrolling in an independent study unit under my supervision.

The Department of Education supported the project by approving the release of preschool and primary teachers for a two-hour meeting each month from February through December. Margaret Reidl, the principal education officer (early childhood), led us through the procedures necessary for approval and joined me in visiting the principals of the schools involved to explain the project and make arrangements for staff release. She also chose to become a fully participating member of the seminar.

As I had done in South Australia, I established criteria for inviting teachers to participate: (1) they were already beginning to use play as the basis for programming, (2) they were open to new ideas, willing to experiment and take risks, (3) they were able to reflect on their reading and practice, and (4) they wanted to increase their awareness of how to use play as a vehicle for children's learning. The teachers had come to my attention as I visited child care centers, preschools, and primary classrooms while supervising university students on practicum. All of them were doing outstanding work with children; the classroom atmosphere and energy immediately conveyed, Whatever is happening here is best for children! I checked my impressions with Lyn and Margaret before approaching the teachers; they agreed that these teachers were examples of good practice.

I invited six teachers to join the project group, explaining that I wanted a commitment from them over the year. All six accepted the challenge. They included a child care director with many years' experience; a child care worker with three years' experience who had just finished her Associate Diploma and wanted something to keep her challenged; two very experienced preschool teachers; a teacher of five- and six-year-olds; and a master teacher who had pioneered mixed-age grouping with a class of five- to nine-year-olds, and who also occasionally had visitors from the preschool and from the remedial class. All of their principals agreed to their participation, and their staff teams became, to varying degrees, receivers of or enthusiastic participants in the teachers' experiments with play programming in their classrooms.

In the following weeks several other teachers asked if they could participate too. In retrospect I believe I should have welcomed them, but at the time I believed that it was safer to proceed on a smaller scale, so I refused them.

Nancy P. ALexander

Staff development strategies

As in South Australia, teacher participation was voluntary. We were inviting teachers to read, experiment in their classrooms, observe, attend monthly meetings, and contribute their insights as co-investigators. All of us were interested in increasing our understanding of play. In addition, Margaret, Lyn, and I were committed to supporting the professional growth of the adults involved. I was consciously implementing, and demonstrating for colleagues, an in-service model of action research in which collaborative inquiry serves as the vehicle for teacher growth.

At our first meeting we agreed that Lyn and I would visit each center early in the project to videotape play episodes. The surprisingly high quality of the play we saw reminded us how strong is the predisposition to play in childhood. We were able to use these videos in our seminars to analyze and compare

children's play as well as to acquaint the teachers with each other's settings.

At our meetings we watched parts of the videos and a film on sociodramatic play, discussed our reading and swapped books and articles, and shared our observations of play episodes. We found that a good deal of debriefing time was needed after each intervening month and that the most important time was that given to participants to share what they had done and what they had observed children doing. The fact that the participants originally had little knowledge of each other's settings seemed to contribute to their interest in hearing about each other's experiences.

From the beginning of the year, teachers were excited about the ideas for provisioning for pretend play that they got from their readings and from each other. Between meetings they tried out new play

---

Where funding is available for substitutes, or where other coverage can be provided, teachers can be offered the added incentive of meetings held on paid time. Collaboration between the university and the department of education enabled this group of teachers to meet monthly during working hours.

themes based on children's experiences. Most play themes were highly successful, as indicated by children's instant interest and by their extension of the play over longer-than-usual times. The play was not packed up at the end of a session but allowed to continue from day to day or week to week.

Throughout the year we emphasized observation. We asked teachers to set up opportunities for sociodramatic play and then step back, once a week for up to 10 minutes, to record a play episode in as much detail as possible. The value of the observations was twofold: (1) they required teachers to look closely and record accurately what children were doing, and (2) they helped teachers to name the play honestly, instead of assuming that they knew what children were doing and learning. Teachers commented that observing was one of the very positive outcomes of the project. It was demanding, they found, but it enabled them to see and hear so much more.

Teachers found various ways of making it clear that they were observing and therefore could not deal with children's requests. Some simply ignored the children. Some explained that they were busy observing and must not be interrupted. One wore a hat that indicated that the teacher was doing her important observing. Whatever their method, the teachers seemed able to keep interruptions to a minimum, and it was clear that children grow in their understanding of this role. "Did you get that?" asked one child, turning to the observer and pointing to her notepad.

In addition to sharing teachers' on-the-spot observations, we watched selected video episodes together and collaborated in the development of a format for recording them under four headings: the scene, the script, the action, and the social setting. All six teachers experimented with and refined this observation format, and during the year a large number of play episodes were recorded, providing the research team with a quantity of data to be further analyzed.

We asked teachers to read between sessions and provided books and articles to be borrowed. Because the value of play is questioned in many settings, teachers often capitulate in the face of criticism. We saw it as essential that teachers learn to justify the changes they were making; being able to quote authorities is a useful strategy for this purpose. In fact, our discussions proved especially exciting when teachers had seen children behaving in ways that their readings had described. Theory and practice coming together reinforced the teachers' belief that the changes they were making in their practice were positive for children.

Problems in the process

The project design assumed highly motivated teachers with time for reading and program planning and sufficient confidence to participate actively in discussion and mutual questioning. For the most part, this is what we had. Three of the teachers had 10 to 20 years' experience, and a fourth had more than 6; all were solid in their teaching skills and their commitment to play. The two child care staff were younger, each in her third year of teaching, but they were bright and questioning and responsive to support. We lost one group member, the child care director, when she was promoted to another administrative position; and her replacement, a young teacher, did not attend regularly. She was busy with her new responsibilities and had missed the initial experience of the group's coming together.

One of the primary teachers had been ambivalent about joining the group because of the time commitment involved;

however, during the year she made significant change toward allowing children to build and manage their own play environment, remaining unflappable in the midst of the action in a class of 30 children (sometimes combined with another teacher's class of 30). In contrast, one of the experienced preschool teachers made few changes in her practice and was uninterested in continuing for a second year when this was proposed by other members of the group.

Some of the teachers were in control of their programs and able to make any changes they chose. Others had to modify their practice more slowly, hoping that their staff teams would see the positive aspects of sociodramatic play and support the changes they were making. The young teacher of two- to five-year-olds in child care worked with a staff of untrained women who believed strongly in cleanliness and didn't approve of play. They were a real challenge for the teacher, who wailed in one of our meetings, "Why me? Why me? I can't do this." She thrived with our encouragement, however, and at the end of the year she said to me, "Now I believe in it as much as you do." She was eager to continue the group for a second year.

For the most part, teachers did the reading and observations we asked for and found these resources, together with mutual support, very important. Even the 20-year preschool veteran told us that she still gets anxious when questioned by parents; she asked us for written material that she could show to parents to defend

her program. The more she gave the direction and control of play to the children, the more she felt the need to convince parents that she was not abrogating her teaching responsibilities.

I also had to convince my colleague, Lyn, that I was not abrogating my responsibilities. I had studied play in depth and was committed to its importance, whereas Lyn was curious, but at first skeptical, about the value of play. I wanted to share the leadership role with her, but it is my style to be a low-key facilitator of others' learning. In addition, I was philosophically committed to involving teachers fully in the construction of shared knowledge. While much is known and has been written about play, there is still much to be learned, and I am very much a learner. I expected to learn as much from teachers as they might learn from me; I was dependent on their daily experiences with children to provide data for my continuing thinking. I anticipated that our sharing would give the teachers feelings of greater confidence and power.

Lyn was different in both her knowledge and her personal style. She was keen to talk about her reading and thinking, and she tended to lead from the front when I wanted the teachers to feel that they were taking the lead. A science educator, Lyn is a fine logical thinker and observer, and she helps me think things through. Our different frames of mind made us a good learning team; they also created issues of shared leadership that had to be worked out in the course of the year.

Finding our voices

Teachers in their classrooms are both too busy to reflect on their practice and, typically, too isolated intellectually; they are doers rather than thinkers. The project seminar met only once a month, but its importance to the teachers was clear. Their need to tell what had been happening for them dominated the beginning—and beyond—of every meeting. By beginning our first seminar with an hour of introductions, we set the stage for this continued sharing. We not only raised many issues that were to recur during the year, we also made it clear that teachers' voices were what we most wanted to hear.

As in traditional college classes, we offered book and film discussions, and our videotaped observations served both to introduce the teachers to each other's settings and to provide commonly experienced play episodes for us to think about together; but the heart of our work together was teachers' own observations. We made it clear that participants' experiences and ideas were the most important content of the seminars. We insisted that taking time out to observe was a legitimate and necessary part of teaching. And in her final evaluation of the experience, one teacher wrote simply, "The best thing you made us do is spend ten minutes a week observing."

Teachers' words and experiences were shared publicly, as well. The teachers were instrumental in planning and presenting a series of two seminars at which they presented information and outcomes of the project. These took place at the university in February and March of the year following the project. The first seminar, on the importance and value of play, discussed research into sociodramatic play by Smilansky (1971) and Fein (1987), and we viewed and discussed a film on sociodramatic play (Lindbergh & Moffatt, 1972). The second seminar included clips from our videos and a panel of three teachers speaking about their play programs and how the project influenced their understanding and practice.

I quoted teachers extensively in my written project report, copies of which went to the university; the Territory Department of Education; colleagues in my "play" network; and the project participants, who were acknowledged by name. Toward the end of the project year, I approached the Northern Territory Children's Services Resource and Advisory

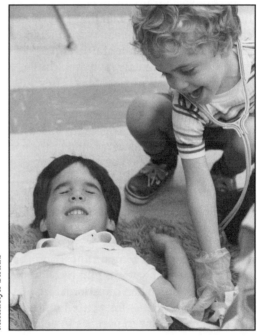

Michaelyn Straub

Program with a proposal that it underwrite the production of six in-service kits based on our project experience. These kits translate our whole experience into a guide for staff development in child care centers. The kits can be used by a teaching team to take its members through the process of our project: observing, reading, analyzing, and evaluating.

For several reasons our plan to continue the project into a second year with a larger and more diverse group was not implemented, but three of our six original participants decided to continue meeting on their own, moving ahead to a new challenge in which they would compare the emergent curriculum that arises from children's interests to the prescribed curriculum guidelines for preschool and the early years of school.

As we keep discovering, teachers who have found a voice keep talking to each other.

What was taught, what was learned, and what are the implications?

Both projects described here—Preschoolers and Print, and Play Programming in Early Childhood Settings—grew out of educators' compelling questions about theory and practice in early childhood education. In each, a colleague and I sought teachers to engage with us in action research designed to discover whether a selected theory worked in the real world of programs for young children.

We asked teachers to observe children and to represent their experiences in words—oral and written—and in images—videos, photographs, and samples of children's creations. For children and adults alike, *representations* of experiences make those experiences available for continued reflection and dialogue.

In each project the data we collected together confirmed and extended our theoretical understanding, empowered teachers as knowers, and generated ideas and resources for teacher education. We discovered early in the play project, for example, how much and how well children would play if given some encouragement; and by the end of the year, we were most excited by the fact that a program based in sociodramatic play seemed to suit all of the children observed, from two to nine years of age. One child care teacher declared that every child would play in the sociodramatic mode if given an appropriate environment and adult support. The teacher of five- to nine-year-olds allowed two hours daily for sociodramatic play and found that she was able to facilitate a high level of learning during these times.

Such discoveries by teachers addressed my own motivation for initiating this project. Teaching university students to understand that sociodramatic play is a crucial vehicle through which children learn how to make their way in the world, I had found few early childhood settings where students, on their practicum, would see children learning through play. I knew if I could discover

Teachers who find their voices in small, safe groups become increasingly confident speaking up in less comfortable settings. Growing leadership among colleagues—at work and in such public settings as workshops and conferences—is to be expected, although not required, of teachers empowered through this approach. The "ripple effect" spreading out from voluntary groups involving relatively few teachers has potential, over time, for wider and wider circles of influence.

how to influence practice in schools and child care centers, I would be able to offer more appropriate practicum experience for my students. The projects I've described taught me how this might be done.

For further information

Creaser, B.H. (1987). *An examination of the four-year-old "master dramatist."* Unpublished master's project, Pacific Oaks College, Pasadena, CA.

Creaser, B.H. (1990). *Play programming in early childhood settings: Action Research Project* (unpublished report). Darwin, NT: Northern Territory University.

Creaser, B.H. (1990, December). *Pretend play: A natural path to learning.* Watson, ACT: Australian Early Childhood Resource Booklets No. 5.

Creaser, B.H. (1990, September). *Rediscovering pretend play.* Watson, ACT: Australian Early Childhood Resource Booklets No. 4.

Creaser, B.H., & Parsons, K. (1988). Preschoolers and print: An Australian teachers' project. In E. Jones (Ed.), *Reading, writing and talking with four, five and six year olds.* Pasadena, CA: Pacific Oaks College.

Other suggested readings

Almy, M., Monighan, P., Scales, B., & Van Hoorn, J. (1984). Recent research on play: The perspective of the teacher. In L. Katz (Ed.), *Current topics in early childhood education: Vol. 5.* (pp. 1–25). Norwood, NJ: Ablex.

Bettelheim, B. (1987, March). The importance of play. *The Atlantic,* pp. 35–46.

Clay, M. (1975). *What did I write?* Portsmouth, NH: Heinemann.

Clemens, S.G. (1983). *The sun's not broken, a cloud's just in the way.* Mt. Rainier, MD: Gryphon House.

Crowe, B. (1983). *Play is a feeling.* London: Allen and Unwin.

Dyson, A.H. (1990). Research in review. Symbol makers, symbol weavers: How children link play, pictures, and print. *Young Children, 45*(2), 50–57.

Goodman, Y. (1980). The roots of literacy. In M.P. Douglas (Ed.), *The Claremont Reading Conference 44th Yearbook* (pp. 1–32). Claremont, CA: Claremont Graduate School.

Hawkins, F.P. (1986). *The logic of action.* Boulder: Colorado Universities Press.

Holdaway, D. (1979). *The foundations of literacy.* Portsmouth, NH: Heinemann.

Humphrey, S. (1989). Becoming a better kindergarten teacher: The case of myself. *Young Children, 45*(1), 16–22.

Isenberg, J., & Quisenberry, N.L. (1988). Play: A necessity for all children. *Childhood Education, 64*(3), 138–145.

Jones, E., & Reynolds, G. (1992). *The play's the thing: Teachers' roles in children's play.* New York: Teachers College Press.

Moyles, J.R. (1989). *Just playing.* Milton-Keynes, UK: Open University Press.

Paley, V.G. (1984). *Boys and girls: Superheroes in the doll corner.* Chicago: University of Chicago Press.

Paley, V.G. (1986). *Mollie is three: Growing up in school.* Chicago: University of Chicago Press.

Schickedanz, J. (1986). *More than the ABCs: The early stages of reading and writing.* Washington, DC: NAEYC.

Teale, W.H. (1983). Toward a theory of how children learn to read and write naturally. *Language Arts, 59*(9), 555–570.

Van Hoorn, J., Nourot, P., Scales, B., & Alward, K. (1993). *Play at the center of the curriculum.* New York: Merrill/Macmillan.

Wasserman, S. (1990). *Serious players in the primary classroom.* New York: Teachers College Press.

References

Fein, G. (1987). Pretend play. In D. Gorlitz & J.F. Wohlwill (Eds.), *Curiosity, imagination and play.* Hillsdale, NJ: Erlbaum.

Lindbergh, L., & Moffatt, M. (1972). *Dramatic play: An integrative approach* [Film]. New York: Campus Films.

Smilansky, S. (1971). Can adults facilitate play in children? Theoretical and practical considerations. In N. Curry & S. Arnaud (Eds.), *Play: The child strives for self-realization.* Washington, DC: NAEYC.

To contact the author, write
Barbara Creaser, 1 Manchester Court, 31 Barlow Street, Scullin, A.C.T. 2614, Australia. *Note:* The kits mentioned in this chapter are in preparation; contact the author for information about them.

A ll of these stories make it clear that external facilitators can make an important contribution to staff development in early childhood education. But where can such facilitators be found? One approach, supporting experienced teachers as peer mentors, is described in the following account of a project developed at Palo Alto Children's Health Council. As previously mentioned, both Mountain View Center and the Pasadena Partnership Project, in expanding to include Head Start, also involved experienced teachers in working with other teachers.

In the final chapter of this book, the question of finding and growing facilitators will be discussed in greater depth.

Chapter 8

I'll Visit Your Class, You Visit Mine: Experienced Teachers as Mentors

Lisa Poelle

Lisa Poelle

_____ **Mentors Share Their Stories*** _____

Each week the first half of the mentor seminar was spent in updating each other on situations that had been developing with their interns. Today Marianne told about an especially memorable observation time at her intern's center. She had spent nearly an hour doing a running observation of Georgia, the intern, writing down everything involving Georgia including all of her dialogue with children. During their conference time immediately afterward, Georgia read these notes with delight. She was able to see the reasons behind the children's behaviors: "So that's why Jason was so fussy..." "I thought Julie had the car first...."

_____
*Here the storyteller is Lisa Poelle, describing a meeting of the mentor seminar she led weekly for a group of experienced early childhood teachers serving as mentors for teachers (called "interns" in this mentor teacher project) in other centers.

For the first time Georgia got a sense of the child's experience from the *child's* point of view. Because of the level of detail in the notes, she was able to understand how certain words or movements of adults affect what happens next with children. She had been introduced to the possibility of *reflecting* on her experience. The mentors discussed the importance of learning to do observations like this, and all of them made plans to make such observations of their interns and, in turn, to ask their interns to write observations of their mentors. A level of trust had developed that made this kind of sharing possible.

Cristina described a conflict that erupted between two boys in her intern's preschool classroom. The intern tried to talk to the boys but became increasingly frustrated. She glanced at Cristina for moral support, and Cristina offered to step in. Using social problem-solving techniques, she was able to help the children define the problem and generate alternative solutions. The intern was extremely grateful for this demonstration; she had never seen anyone handle a conflict so expertly! She talked to Cristina for a long time, saying that she could do that, too, now that she knew what it looked like.

Another intern, Debbie, had requested ideas for circle time because she had a hard time keeping the children interested. Observing at her mentor's center, she watched closely how her mentor worked with the large group, and on occasion she took over a group time at her mentor's center. This gave her a chance to try things with a group that had no preconceived notions about her abilities. Her confidence grew enormously, and she increased her repertoire substantially. Eventually she tried these activities at her own center while the mentor observed. Because Debbie had established trust in the mentor, she didn't feel nervous and was able to ask for suggestions for improvement, which she genuinely appreciated.

Mentors also talked about days that weren't going so well when the intern observed at the mentor's center. The interns' response was always, "I'm so glad to see that your room isn't perfect." When one child vomited, another had a nosebleed, and everyone else was making the transition to snack time, the room was absolutely chaotic, and the intern leaped into action, taking over snack-time duties. She later told the mentor that it felt good to be able "to give something back."

The setting

As a child care consultant for the Children's Health Council of Palo Alto, California, I had frequent opportunities to model certain techniques for teachers in their classrooms. I became increasingly aware of the value of simply watching another skilled adult work effectively with children. I also discovered that while some teachers have access to a knowledgeable director or coteacher who can provide them with personal and useful feedback to their questions, many new teachers lack a strong support system. They may be team teaching with someone who is also fairly new to the field. Their director may not have time to offer regular feedback and personal support.

Concurrently, I saw that a good many veteran teachers were leaving the field after spending many years developing their expertise. Some were frustrated with the steady stream of new teachers who required substantial training and then moved on after only a few months on the job. Some felt taken for granted by parents and co-workers. They believed that they had reached the top of the career ladder, unless they went on to become directors— and that would mean leaving the children.

I began thinking about what could be done to address the dilemmas of both new and veteran teachers. I asked the following questions:

• How can we honor the excellence of our veteran teachers?

• How can we create a new rung on the career ladder for these experienced teachers?

• How can we stem the turnover among new teachers who become frustrated with so much responsibility after so little training and ongoing support?

• Could these needs be addressed by arranging ways for teachers to help each other?

I set out to develop a program that would enable knowledgeable and highly skilled veteran teachers to develop a gratifying and mutually beneficial relationship with committed and enthusiastic new teachers and with each other, as well. The outcome was a proposal for a mentor teacher program that I asked the Children's Health Council to sponsor.

Children's Health Council is a 40-year-old, multidisciplinary, private, nonprofit agency dedicated to serving children and their families by providing a variety of diagnostic, therapeutic, and educational services. While its primary focus is on children with special needs, it has also, over a 10-year period, provided more than 300 hours per year of consultation and staff training on site at child care centers in the area, at little or no cost to parents or staff. Because of the never-ending need for such service created by the high rate of staff turnover in child care centers, a proposal for an innovative, cost-effective approach to the problem of providing child care consultation was welcomed by the agency staff and, ultimately, by foundations to which we applied for support. The letter from the Children's Health Council directors that accompanied our funding request summed up the project as follows:

> The concept is simple. Each semester, eight experienced and skillful child care teachers will be selected and matched

with eight enthusiastic, bright, but inexperienced child care teachers in different centers. The experienced teachers will observe, consult, support, and mentor the new teachers. Both groups will gain in skills and job satisfaction. The Children's Health Council will provide the training and ongoing supervision of the mentors through biweekly seminars. Over a two-year period 32 mentor teachers will develop consultant skills, which they in turn can share with their own centers and others in the child care community. In this way the available pool of skilled child care consultants will be expanded. A secondary but no less important gain will be the increased job satisfaction of the participating mentors and teachers, which hopefully will increase their likelihood of remaining in the field. While the "mentor" concept is well known in business and is currently being developed in the public schools, it is a new concept for child care programs. We believe that this innovative program has potential for replication in many communities throughout the nation. Our staff plans to develop conference presentations as well as written materials for distribution.

The project recruited participants from the dozen communities within a 30-minute drive of the council, on the San Francisco peninsula between San Francisco and San Jose. Although this area includes a wide socioeconomic range and some racial diversity, project participants were primarily White and middle class.

Building the mentoring network

To contact teachers who might choose to become mentors or interns, we sent information packets and application forms to 50 local child care directors. We decided to go through directors because they would need to "nominate" teachers for the program and give them release time for doing observations in the other teacher's center. Because many of the directors had previously used the council's consultation services, we believed that we would get a good response. With follow-up phone calls as well, we received 19 applications within six weeks—9 for intern positions and 10 for mentor positions.

Applicants were asked to list their past work experience and education and to respond to four essay questions. Potential mentors were asked the following:

1. What do you see as important components of high-quality child care?

2. Who has influenced your style of teaching and/or theory of child development (authors, instructors, co-workers, etc.)? How? What did you learn from them? Please be as specific as possible.

3. Describe your past experience in working with new teachers. What did you enjoy? What did you find frustrating?

4. Why do you want to be a part of this program?

Potential interns were asked these questions:

1. Why did you choose to work in this field?

2. Think of the best teacher you know. What is it about him or her that you admire?

3. As a teacher, what do you currently see as your main areas of strength?

4. In what areas would you like help and new ideas?

Our plan was to review the applications and then to visit each applicant's center

for an hour to observe the teacher in action with children. Visits would give us an opportunity to view the classroom setting and gather information about the teacher's style, personality, and competence. Questions in an observation guide asked for the observer's impressions of the applicant's interactions with children, with other staff, and with parents; her intervention in a conflict situation; and the overall environment. Paper screening, paired observations, and final screening and matching were done by the volunteer members of a selection committee, of which I was also a member.

We eliminated three mentor applicants through the paper screening; one had less than five years' teaching experience; one was a director without regular teaching duties; and one answered the essay questions very poorly, giving us the impression of poor communications skills and limited theoretical background. Following observations, we met to match up the candidates. Our plan was to have two categories: infant-toddler teachers and preschool teachers. We screened out as mentors an experienced preschool teacher now working with infants, who had not yet developed confidence with this age level, and a kindergarten teacher for whom no suitable match could be found. We screened out as interns two of three applicants from the same classroom and an applicant with 14 years' experience, whose behavior with children was cursory and custodial (her director had told her to apply because she "needed the training").

We tried to match interns and mentors by personality, needs/strengths, logistics, and the age groups they were currently working with. As it turned out, we needed to find another infant-toddler intern for an outstanding infant-toddler mentor candidate. I described our dilemma to the mentor, who gave us the name of an acquaintance who might be interested. We contacted this person, who was indeed interested, and made arrangements to observe her. Luckily the match was a good one. We settled on a final group of two infant-toddler mentoring couples and four preschool mentoring couples. Together they represented a wide variety of program types—employer supported, church affiliated, private nonprofit, proprietary, and state funded.*

Mentors received a stipend of $500 for the semester. Interns were invited to enroll for three semester units of credit from the local community college, Cañada College. The project also reimbursed centers for hiring substitutes to make the observations possible.

An orientation meeting was held at Children's Health Council for mentoring couples to get acquainted and to plan their initial observation times at each other's centers. Spirits were high as we launched this new program.

Staff development strategies

The plan was for alternating weekly visits of one and a half hours, first by the mentor to her intern's center and then by the intern to her mentor's center. Weekly one-and-a-half hour conferences were arranged so that the mentor and the intern could discuss the observations and other questions of mutual interest. Some couples decided to meet over dinner, others for an extended lunch break. In addition the mentors had a biweekly late-afternoon meeting with me—our mentor seminar.

The intensive observation schedule provided a wealth of stories about children's and teachers' experiences in the classroom. Mentors took notes that they shared with interns. Interns watched their

---

*Later mentor-intern groups also included part-day preschools and family day care.

mentors in action with children, asked questions, and had opportunities to see both good and bad moments in someone else's classroom. By their questions and their efforts to model their own behavior on their mentor's, interns reflected and validated the mentors' work. By their observations and comments, mentors reflected, validated, and provided new possibilities for the interns as growing teachers. It became evident that the regular presence in one's classroom of another teacher with whom one has a relationship serves as affirmation of the importance and reality of one's daily work: Someone other than me knows and cares about what I'm doing. Participants found it especially meaningful to have someone appreciate the subtleties of their craft. Quality child care can be such a quiet accomplishment.

In my consulting I have been conscious of my responsibility as an expert; my role is to provide information to child care centers that have asked for help. Because I had this in mind as I designed the mentor seminars that I was to lead, I divided each seminar into two parts: sharing/problem solving and content/presentation. Most of our time would be devoted to talking about relationships: mentor/intern, teacher/child, teacher/teacher, and teacher/administrator. I planned to introduce discussion content on individual differences in temperament, management of behavior problems, and the role of the teacher during free play. In addition I arranged for talks by several clinicians from Children's Health Council who had broadened my own understanding of children's development and behavior. I hoped to add another dimension for the mentors by addressing what appeared to be a void in most teachers' educational backgrounds: a working knowledge of developmental "red flags" and understanding of the therapeutic intervention process. As a representative of Children's

Elisabeth Nichols

Health Council, I had often encountered, even in experienced and mature teachers, a lack of knowledge in these areas.

We began our first mentor seminar by listening to descriptions of each classroom setting, mentors' and interns', in order to form "pictures" for ourselves. As each person shared her recent experiences, feelings of enthusiasm were mixed with feelings of confusion about the mentor role. While everyone *believed* in the concept of mentoring, no one had ever before been involved in a relationship formed solely for that purpose. Mentors weren't sure how "directive" to be with their interns. They thought of themselves mainly as responders to questions and requests for help—as facilitators in a process initiated by the intern. Some interns had made things easier for the mentors by bringing clear-cut issues to conference times, but others seemed to rely on the mentor to supply them with topics for discussion.

I encouraged the mentors to structure the conference times as loosely or as formally as they found necessary, depending on the intern's contribution. They could choose to begin by simply sharing what they observed in each other's classrooms, describing interesting play, language, child behavior, and so forth. I also suggested sharing stories about children from their own present or past teaching experiences that might relate to the intern's stories in the here-and-now.

Each week the first half of the seminar was spent in updating each other on situations that had been developing in the various centers. Sometimes the mentors talked about issues they had been discussing with their interns. Sometimes they talked more about their own centers' issues and the struggles they were having personally. Just as the mentor-intern conferences were opportunities for storytelling about interns' new progress as teachers, the mentor seminars were opportunities for mentors to share their own stories about teaching with this group of peers. The group developed into a sensitive and supportive "oasis," as one mentor put it.

Unanticipated consequences

Directors' reactions

Problems that arose out of the design of the mentor program reflected the extent to which center directors had been "left out of the loop." While we contacted directors to recruit mentors and interns, we had no further planned contact with them until midway through the semester, when I hosted a luncheon for them. The purpose of this luncheon was to thank them for their support, to offer a chance for them to do some networking, and to get feedback on the program from a director's point of view. I especially wanted to know if they were dissatisfied with any part of the program so that I could make the necessary changes.

Most comments were glowing; interns and mentors had told their directors wonderful things about their experience. All directors said they would be willing to participate again with another teacher. Several of the interns' directors, however, were uneasy about someone's "judging" their program based on the performance of a novice teacher. As we talked it became apparent that at the beginning of each semester, the mentoring pair should meet with the intern's director to allow her to explain the philosophy of the center. Directors simply do not trust the intern to explain the operation and philosophy of the center adequately.

During this discussion it became clear to me that there were other underlying issues. Some directors sponsored interns because they had certain training goals in mind. They really wanted to be able to take the mentor aside and tell her what the intern should be working on. The goal of the program, however, was to enable people to be self-directed in their learning. It was frustrating for these directors to be so impotent in relation to the program.

I believe that I heard some jealousy voiced by a few directors. The mentors and interns had developed a very special and intimate relationship. It seemed to me that most directors would love the opportunity to nurture and support their staff the way mentors can do, but their job doesn't usually allow enough time to develop that kind of closeness.

I saw the content of the mentor-intern conference as "emergent curriculum for adults." This was explained to the directors at the beginning of the program, and their response was that they were happy to offer this "perk" to their novice teachers; but as the interns showed signs of growth and self-confidence, some directors seemed to want to participate in the "fine-tuning" efforts. When they saw that the mentor had been able to help the intern, they wanted to use the mentor as a tool for their own agenda.

It seems likely that directors' uneasy feelings stem from a disruption of the hierarchy. The mentor program presents an interesting dilemma for the intern's director; you can get a personal coach/trainer for a promising new teacher, but you and your center give up a certain amount of privacy and control. By allowing this new teacher to observe elsewhere, you risk losing her to a more appealing center. New teachers are more prone to relocating; their loyalty is not firmly established and they may be still "testing the waters."

For effective directors confident of their center's quality, this risk may not be apparent. Two of the directors who felt very comfortable with the structure of the mentor program explained that they would want to relay information to the mentor only through the intern. The mentor-intern relationship should be private; directors should definitely not give input on goal setting. This program, they believed, was a way for new teachers to share their insecurities and questions with someone without fear of affecting their performance evaluations and raises. The principle of external facilitation was clearly one that they understood.

Leaving jobs

The directors least comfortable with the program structure were, understandably, those whose interns were critical of their centers. The stickiest situation, which raised a dilemma for all of us, involved an intern who became so disillusioned with her own center during the course of the semester that she wanted to quit her job and apply for a job opening in her

An early childhood mentor program...

Offers interns

1. a nonevaluative relationship with a master teacher from another program;

2. an opportunity for regular observation of a skilled teacher at work in her own classroom;

3. an opportunity to be regularly observed and get positive feedback and personal support;

4. perspective on the programs in which they work; and

5. support for risk taking and speaking up.

Offers mentors

1. affirmation as master teachers of children;

2. new challenges to practice their skills in working with adults, with potential spin-off beyond the intern relationship;

3. professional network building through regular discussions with peers in the mentor seminar;

4. new information for their professional growth;

5. perspective on the programs in which they work; and

6. support for risk taking and speaking up.

Offers directors

1. intensive support for a staff member's growth—in the role of intern or mentor;

2. an opportunity for a new teacher to experience a nonevaluative growth relationship;

3. the stimulation of an observer's presence in the center;

4. an opportunity for professional networking; and

5. the risk of greater teacher assertiveness.

mentor's center. She had been trying to reconcile differences in teaching styles with her co-worker, but her efforts had proven futile. She felt that the director was not being supportive and that there was no hope of working things out.

This was disturbing news to me; I believed that her director would blame my program for causing her to lose a teacher. It would look as though the mentor "stole" the intern away from her center.

We discussed this problem at length at the seminar. The intern had been exposed to a "master teacher"—her mentor. Her eyes had been opened to the kind of child-oriented, developmentally appropriate practice that characterizes skillful interaction with young children. While she endeavored to model herself after this person, she began to see the flaws in her own co-teacher's approach. It got harder and harder for the intern to tolerate the philosophical differences, and she had no success in resolving those differences through staff meetings or conferences with the director.

When the opening came up in the mentor's classroom, it was like a dream-come-true for the intern. She wanted to apply for the position, but she did not want to jeopardize the mentor program by doing so.

I asked the mentor if the intern would consider waiting to resign until after the semester ended. If she left prior to the end, we would have to drop that pair from the program because the conditions of their relationship and the locations would be changed. This plan might work if the intern were indeed hired by the mentor's center and if that center would agree to hold the job open until the end of the semester.

As it turned out this plan did work. The intern gave her notice but agreed to stay until the end of the semester. The other center interviewed her and hired her to come aboard after the program ended. The director of the intern's center was not happy with this outcome, but she was glad to have two months to find a replacement.

At first I was disappointed that one of "my" interns had not experienced "increased job satisfaction" due to this program, as my goals stated; however, it turns out that the intern has found a center that is a better match for her philosophically. She now has increased job satisfaction and, although it meant leaving her original center, she is more likely to remain in the field because she is happier at her job.

By the end of the semester, another intern had decided to leave her job. She had been struggling with her director over

---

Teachers Work With Other Adults, As Well As With Children

Professional early childhood educators typically lack a theoretical base for working with adults, even though they often teach as members of a team. A continuing support group focused on adult relationships can address significant issues:

1. team-teaching conflicts

2. problems in making systems work

3. disagreements with administration

4. coping with change

philosophical differences and policy decisions all year. The issues were mainly those involving contact with parents. This intern was actually the head teacher in her room. She had talked with her mentor about often feeling powerless in developing stronger parent-teacher relationships because of the policies that called for director-parent conferencing, excluding the teachers. Certain situations had come up during the semester that had created communication problems for the intern, and she had shared those with her mentor. The mentor offered support and guidance in trying to resolve the issues, but to no avail. By the end of the program, the intern had given notice to her director. She actually took several months off, trying to decide if she even wanted to stay in the field. In the end she applied for and accepted a position at her mentor's center, even though the mentor had since left to go to graduate school.

© Robert Bowie

This intern chose to stay in the field because, through observations in the mentor program, she had been exposed to a center that practiced high-quality child care and strong staff support. She had a broader sense of what the field had to offer because she had the opportunity to see new things.

While the director was not happy at this turn of events, I believe that these kinds of changes are good for the field as a whole. If teachers leave over program-quality issues, then it can be hoped that the administrators will take a fresh look at their programs. Good teachers are hard to replace.

Adult relationship issues

I hadn't anticipated that the majority of the conferencing times would be spent talking about program issues involving adults—team-teaching conflicts, systems problems, disagreements with administration, staffing changes, and so on. I had

thought that most of the time would be spent discussing problems related to children, probably because that had been the number-one request in my consultation work. It is clear, however, that new teachers have a real need to talk about the issues that arise out of the process of collaboration.

People have strong opinions about how children should be cared for. Coming to some kind of agreement is not always easy. Issues of control and competition enter too many centers, making the child's needs secondary to the staff's needs. Through this project I found that new teachers as well as veteran teachers are constantly being faced with challenges to their professionalism. They need ways to reassess their beliefs, and talking with a supportive colleague is a good way to do that "reality check."

One drawback to having a supportive colleague was that sometimes interns would quote mentors at staff meetings. This was not usually well received by other staff or

> ### Some Characteristics of an Effective Mentor Program
>
> **1.** mutual observation, taking place in the mentor's as well as in the intern's classroom
>
> **2.** follow-up discussion of observations
>
> **3.** a nonevaluative mentor/intern relationship in which the intern, not her director, sets goals for her growth
>
> **4.** careful matching of mentors and interns from programs with similar child populations
>
> **5.** a regular seminar for mentors to discuss issues in working with adults
>
> **6.** ample time in the seminar for mentors to share their stories and questions with one another
>
> **7.** attention to building rapport with center directors, with opportunities to meet, give feedback, and interpret their program to mentors.

by directors. The mentors of these interns solved the problem by asking the interns to be more discreet, voicing their opinions but not giving credit to the mentors.

Empowering teachers

The project empowered interns by supporting risk taking on their part. Interns were more likely to speak up with other staff members at their centers; two decided to apply for jobs at other centers; one intern later became a mentor. Teachers who become more confident and knowledgeable do not necessarily limit their behavioral changes to their interactions with children. They may demand system changes as well.

Similarly, mentors were empowered in their communication skills and their willingness to take risks. Directors commented that their teachers who were mentors had become more tolerant and skillful in relationships with their co-workers. They seemed to have fine-tuned their leadership skills, demonstrating and intervening more smoothly than before. There was also a bonus in the intern's visits, one director remarked: When the intern comes to observe, *everyone* seems to do their best job.

In evaluating their experience in the program, mentors emphasized the importance of being affirmed as professionals.

• "It was a real pleasure to share common territory on equal terms. This opportunity confirmed the professional aspect of my job."

• "Being identified as a 'master-level teacher' was gratifying. I've been feeling taken for granted at my center."

• "This definitely transferred to my job, creating new interest in old things."

• "It made me feel useful to the profession in a totally new way."

• "With the amount of turnover in this field, it was very nice to know that there are other dedicated teachers out there."

One mentor applied again as a mentor for the following semester.

Although each mentor was selected in part for her ability to demonstrate effective caregiving/teaching techniques, not all were used to translating their practice into words. Being asked to articulate reasons for their style of teaching gave mentors an opportunity, in the words of one mentor, "to polish your own mirror." Mentors found themselves speaking with more confidence to parents as well as to staff. Several developed workshop presentations for local conferences.

Like the interns, not all mentors experienced increased satisfaction in their current jobs. Several have moved toward administration or taken initiative in developing new programs. Several have returned to school. One joined Children's Health Council as a child care consultant and took over my position as coordinator of the mentor program in its second year.

What was taught and learned?

Mentor seminars

The mentor seminar was critical to the effectiveness of the program. Mentoring is a difficult concept to grasp. Many questions arise in terms of specific behavior. At times a mentor is passive, listening and observing; at other times she is active, advising and modeling. Deciding which approach will best help the intern requires a high degree of thoughtfulness and excellent interpersonal skills.

When the mentors met together, they talked about situations they were encountering and strategies they were using as they worked toward becoming effective mentors. While I facilitated these discussions, the mentors proved an invaluable resource for each other. They felt confident in their abilities but appreciated the chance to come together to discuss difficult or confusing situations. Issues in working with adults were the primary

focus of discussions, and this was also the case in many of the discussions between mentors and interns. Coming to agreement with co-workers may be a more difficult challenge than working effectively with young children.

Mentors were stimulated by the professional level of the discussions; they had found like-minded colleagues with whom they could discuss their field. Many had been out of school for some years and were refreshed by involvement in a new educational program. They devoured advanced-level child development information given by me or other speakers, and all of us shared with each other resources that we had been collecting for many years. Interns appreciated handouts and curriculum ideas that mentors were able to provide for them, and mentors made good use of materials from the seminar, using them in their own work as much as with the interns.

Observing

The observation component of the program was a major reason for its success. In some other mentor programs, the intern observes the mentor teacher in her classroom and then tries to apply what she has learned in her own class, assessing what she is doing without direct feedback. When the mentor comes to the intern's classroom on a regular basis, however, she really gets to know the children and can directly offer pertinent feedback based on observations made while the intern is absorbed in working with the children. The observer becomes a third eye, a recorder of the big picture. Having someone describe a classroom scene from the periphery and then share it objectively is a rare gift for a teacher. In the mentor program these observations became the foundation for many philosophical as well as practical discussions.

Relationships with directors

We found that the mentor in a child care program needs special sensitivity to center protocol. The mentor-intern relationship has potential for threatening the authority of the intern's director. Stepping into a center as an "expert" disrupts the normal hierarchy that has been established among staff. Mentors must take care to develop some kind of rapport with the director, even though she or he is not directly involved in the mentoring relationship; for example, simply making an effort to sign in and say hello helped to build a connection between mentor and director.

In making revisions in the continuing program, we rewrote the orientation letter to directors, asked mentor-intern pairs to arrange a meeting with the director prior to the first observation, moved up the date of the directors' luncheon, and were explicit in asking that directors be informed of all observation times and be given all handout information. We also added a clause to the agreement form about remaining at the sponsoring center during the program.

Recruiting and matching participants

Recruiting efforts must be sustained. We have made presentations at conferences and community colleges, as well as contacting directors by mail, in order to assure an adequate applicant pool. We also extended our geographic base, accepting applications from anyone willing to make the necessary drive.

Even when the pool is adequate, the complexity of matching pairs has resulted in our never having than six pairs in any semester. It is important, we have found, to match mentors and interns very carefully based on personal schedules, personalities, type of center, and distance

to be traveled. The weekly conferences are crucial to the success of the experience. People have to be compatible for their relationship to flourish. We have also found it necessary to emphasize the role of the mentor as model and support person rather than evaluator. Where one mentor persisted in seeing her role as evaluator, trust and mutual respect never developed.

It is also important to provide each person with a partner working with a similar child population. Mentoring works best when pairs come from centers with similar socioeconomic groups and similar overall structure. Mentors are frequently asked for advice by their interns, and they feel more comfortable offering advice when they are familiar with the type of center and population served. Within the mentor seminar, however, diversity is a positive factor, giving mentors a broader base on which to build new insights about working with children.

In each semester I saw the mentor-intern pairs developing two types of relationships. On one level was the pair who spent the majority of their time sharing curriculum materials and circle-time ideas. They enjoyed observing each other at work and meeting together for the conference. Some even made plans to get together occasionally after the program ended. The interns felt supported and definitely gained new skills, but their level of professional interest was not high. Some were simply overloaded in all areas of their lives. Some were less motivated; they had been encouraged by their directors to participate rather than choosing freely for themselves.

The second type of relationship happened more often. This pair also shared resource materials, but the classroom observations served as a launching pad for looking at the complexity of human behavior. Both teachers sharpened their skills by close study of the interactions between children and adults. They became more articulate in defining developmentally appropriate practice when talking to other teachers or to parents. The intern got into the habit of *thinking* about how she teaches. A high level of trust developed, enabling both intern and mentor to share difficult feelings and struggles within their centers and to feel validated and supported.

Some participants wrote on their evaluation forms that the program helped them to decide to stay in the field. Said one intern,

> When I began the mentor program I was very discouraged and my self-esteem was low. I was wondering why I was even teaching and ready to quit. I was up against many obstacles and had little support. . . . My mentor validated me as a teacher. She gave me the courage; she filled my well; she helped me get direction and enthusiasm. I love my work now. I am at peace and I *know* I am a good teacher!

I believe that this program will continue to be a strong model, showing that individualized training opportunities have a powerful impact in child care. While most traditional teacher-training programs offer information in an adult classroom setting, apart from the children, this program uses real-life situations with customized feedback. It provides a "practicum" for the new teacher in her own center, with the extra benefit of a master teacher giving advice and support.

Teachers of young children are in different stages of professional development. The most effective training is that which addresses the questions teachers have about their own current work situation. It is important that we develop ways to use our existing resources—those experienced people still actively teaching, who can be role models for a new generation of child care professionals.

*   *   *

The Mentor Teacher Program, which began in 1989, is still alive and well in spring 1993 and has continued to recruit an average of six mentor-intern pairs each semester. Contact Monika Perez, Children's Health Council, 700 Sand Hill Road, Palo Alto, CA 94304, (415) 326-5530.

For further information

Poelle, L. (1992). *The mentor program.* Unpublished master's thesis, Pacific Oaks College, Pasadena, CA.

Poelle, L., Marsh, M., & Nattinger, P. (1990, November). *Child care mentor teacher programs: New opportunities for professional recognition and merit compensation.* Paper presented at the NAEYC Annual Conference, Washington, DC. (Materials available from authors)

Other suggested readings

Bey, T.M., & Holmes, C.T. (Eds.). (1990). *Mentoring: Developing successful new teachers.* Reston, VA: Association of Teacher Educators.

Boston, B.O. (1976). *The sorcerer's apprentice: A case study in the role of the mentor.* Reston, VA: Council for Exceptional Children.

Daloz, L.A. (1986). *Effective teaching and mentoring.* San Francisco: Jossey-Bass.

Fagan, M.M., & Walter, G. (1982). Mentoring among teachers. *Journal of Educational Research, 76*(2), 113–118.

Greenman, J.T., & Fuqua, R.W. (1984). *Making day care better: Training, evaluation, and the process of change.* New York: Teachers College Press.

Howey, K. (1988). Mentor-teachers as inquiring professionals. *Theory into Practice, 27*(3), 209–213.

Johnston, J.M. (1984, March). Assessing staff problems: Key to effective staff development. *Child Care Information Exchange, 36,* 19–22.

Jorde-Bloom, P. (1988). *A great place to work: Improving conditions for staff in young children's programs.* Washington, DC: NAEYC.

Katz, L.M. (1977). *Talks with teachers: Reflections on early childhood education.* Washington, DC: NAEYC.

Lambert, D. (1985). Mentor teachers as change facilitators. *Thrust for Educational Leadership, 14*(6), 28–32.

Lowrey, R.G. (1986). *Mentor teachers: The California model.* Bloomington, IN: Phi Delta Kappa Educational Foundation.

Miller, L.M., Thomson, W.A., & Roush, R.E. (1989). Mentorships and the perceived educational payoffs. *Phi Delta Kappan, 70*(6), 465–467.

Odell, S.J. (1990). *Mentor teacher programs.* Washington, DC: National Education Association.

Sheerer, M., & Jorde-Bloom, P. (1990). The ongoing challenge: Attracting and retaining quality staff. *Child Care Information Exchange, 72,* 11–16.

Shulman, J.H. (1988). Look to a colleague. *Instructor, 97*(5), 32–34.

Shulman, J.H., & Colbert, J.A. (1987). *The mentor teacher casebook.* San Francisco: Far West Laboratory for Educational Research and Development.

Spodek, B., Saracho, O.N., & Peters, D.L. (Eds.). *Professionalism and the early childhood practitioner.* New York: Teachers College Press.

Whitebook, M. (Ed.). (1989). *The national child care staffing study executive summary.* Berkeley, CA: Child Care Employee Project.

To contact the author, write Lisa Poelle, Marpoli Associates, Inc., Child Care Consultation and Management, 1105 S. Baywood Avenue, San Jose, CA 95128.

Chapter 9

Looking Back: What We've Learned About Partnerships

Elizabeth Jones

Differences among the projects: Individualized or collective

The projects about which we have told stories have both common themes and significant differences among them. Standing out among the differences is the question, Does the partnership focus only on individual teachers, or does it work to empower them collectively?

All of the partnerships brought groups of teachers together. Some groups were already members of a collective—a school, a school system's preschool programs, or a rural community. Others were, sometimes by design, individuals from different teaching settings meeting temporarily as part of a class or seminar. Typically, participation by teachers in the individualized projects was voluntary; participation in the collectively structured projects was, to some degree, coerced. On a continuum the projects distribute somewhat as the illustration below indicates.

In Boulder and Palo Alto, participation relied on individual teacher initiative. In the Australian projects participation was invitational, and in Darwin several uninvited volunteers were turned away. In Palo Alto a few intern candidates were pushed into the project by their directors, through whom the invitations were distributed; however, such coercion was seen as reducing their potential effectiveness in the project. In the same project, when three staff members from one classroom applied

individualized							*collective*
Boulder / Australia/ Palo Alto / Alaska / Four Corners / Seattle / Pasadena / Soledad							

as interns, two of them were deliberately screened out.

Each of these projects included seminars that built a mutual support group, but this group was separate from teachers' work settings. Teachers could, of course, continue to meet together after the project if they chose, but the probability of that actually happening is low unless building a support network is a conscious part of the project design. It is easy for project designers and facilitators from an individualistic, liberal tradition to overlook the collective side of teacher empowerment.* Most teacher participants in these individualized projects were predictably middle class, White, and relatively secure as individuals in institutional settings.

In Four Corners and Alaska, teacher-participants were individually responsible for preparing CDA portfolios. As members of close-knit Native American communities, however, they worked together as a matter of course ("When Amy and I were working on our portfolios, we encouraged each other. We stayed up all night a few times. . . . "—see Chapter 1). Their work was not undertaken independently; instead, it represented an important contribution to the tribal agency's need to meet national Head Start requirements. The project facilitator did not organize agency staff toward collective action, nor would it have been appropriate for a nonmember of the local community to do so; but cooperative efforts were recognized and encouraged.

In Seattle advisors were assigned to child care centers at the request of center

---

*They are familiar with traditionally independent educational opportunities, including colleges, which leave each applying student on her own. Applicants from college-educated families or college-prep schools aren't actually on their own, however; they have ready access to a whole network of people within "the culture of power" (Delpit, 1988; Lareau, 1989; Rose, 1989).

directors and were generally expected by the director to work with all of the staff. In Pasadena and Soledad the partnerships were initiated by school district administrators, and some requirements for participation were placed on all teachers. In all three settings, however, facilitators countered administrators' expectations by insisting on teacher choice in level of participation. In Alaska the facilitator also insisted on increasing the choices open to Head Start staff.

In each of these collectively structured partnerships, empowerment of teachers to take action beyond the classroom emerged as part of facilitators' work, although it had not been part of the original design. It became clear that teachers' effectiveness in working with children is directly related to their interactions with adults and to their feelings of effectiveness in the larger system, as any union activist could have predicted. Teachers assigned to, rather than individually initiating, participation in a staff development project posed the significant question, "What are 'they' doing to us?" and this question became a recurrent part of the teacher/facilitator agenda. Teacher-participants in the collective partnerships reflected a wide range of ethnic and social-class backgrounds and varied professional experience. Some were sophisticated about the uses of collective action in gaining a vote.

Collective action may take place within a program or beyond it. In Seattle, community networking grew out of facilitators' discouragement with high staff turnover in child care centers. If half of those in whom a facilitator invests energy leave the field every year, action to address more basic needs is called for. The Worthy Wages campaign, which grew out of similar concerns in Seattle and elsewhere, is a program in which NAEYC participates.

In Boulder, with maximum autonomy built in for all participants, advisors prided themselves on "having no predetermined agenda and not imposing or implementing mandated programs" (Apelman, p. 96, this volume). Facilitators in some other partnerships faced greater constraints; they were responsible to national CDA standards in Four Corners and Alaska, to Title VII project objectives in Soledad, and (to an increasingly negotiable extent) to High/Scope curriculum implementation in Pasadena. In Seattle and Palo Alto, some center directors made efforts to get the advisor or mentor to reinforce *their* goals for teachers. In each of these settings, the challenge of working with system expectations enriched the dialogue, creating useful disequilibrium and thus significant construction of knowledge by facilitators, administrators, and teachers.

Facilitation without challenge risks wimpiness. Judith Kleinfeld (1972), analyzing differences in behavioral styles among teachers of Alaska Native high school students, found that teachers who were cool in their interactions with students got relatively low response. Warmth and personal caring were much more effective, but warmth without challenge—laissez-faire teaching—left students unsupported in the hard work of learning. The most effective teachers were identified by Kleinfeld as "supportive gadflies," whose message could be summed up as "I know you can do it, and I expect you to do it because we care about each other" (see also Delpit, 1988). Embedding knowledge in relationship is culturally appropriate for Native Americans as well as for many other learners; it emphasizes collective responsibility and support. It is also appropriate in early childhood staff development (Morgan, 1983; Noddings, 1984).

When facilitation and challenge can come from different, but allied, sources, everyone benefits—including the facilitators and the challengers—if they pay respectful attention to each other's modes of operation. Only within appropriate system constraints—a baseline of required competence—will facilitation work, just as only in a classroom or home with dependable order and limits are children able to make choices that both please them and help them grow.

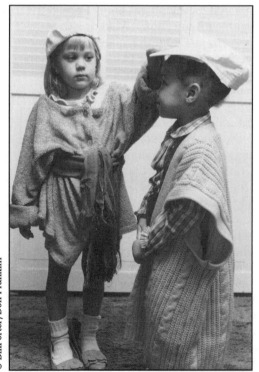

© BmPorter/Don Franklin

Facilitators: Why would an administrator want one around? Risks, losses, and gains

It's hard to be an administrator with a facilitator around. The facilitator has all the fun and gets most of the strokes—as a tradeoff for not having the power. Teachers who have established trust in a facilitator readily use her to facilitate talk, not only about children, but also about system complaints—which often take precedence in teachers' lives over the day-to-day routine with children. Experienced teachers know how to manage their day in the classroom, but "Do you know what SHE did?" is a challenge crying out for a sounding board.

In Pasadena, for example, teachers working within the complex system of a public school district have been quick to say, "No one ever gave us strokes until the partnership came along. All we got was criticism. You've given us confidence in ourselves." Whether this is true or exaggerated, it is more than a matter of cool versus warm personal style, although style may well play a part; rather, it reflects inherent role differences.

"When the principal comes in, he isn't looking for the same things we are looking for," a Boulder teacher said to her facilitator, confidently including her in the "we." Facilitators work on behalf of teachers and are free of system responsibility. Administrators must balance their advocacy for teachers with total-system needs, some of which are inevitably at odds with teachers' perceived needs. "They never tell us anything," teachers complain, not recognizing that it isn't possible to share all administrative decision-making processes, especially those that have to do with

personnel changes and are thus of greatest concern to teachers.

In advocating the truth/love model as an effective approach to organizational management and change (see Chapter 1), Bennis (1976) also makes its limitations clear. Radical restructuring of institutions, he says, never occurs through consensus, only through power—"because people have a terrible time restructuring themselves when they fear that their status, their power, their esteem are going to be lowered" (1976, p. 88). Administrators sometimes must exercise their power, make major changes—and take the flak for it.

"Teaching is not pleasing people. It is opening them to possibilities," Sharon Stine once wrote (Jones, 1983, p. 89). Even more, as Stine made clear in her book on administration (1983), administration is not pleasing people; it is making decisions and taking action while trying to keep possibilities open. Because there is always more action that others want taken than can possibly be addressed, and because others disagree among themselves about what action should be taken, it is very hard to be an administrator and be popular.

It is easy to be a facilitator and be popular with teachers, easy to say yes and not no. It is hard to be a facilitator and be popular with administrators, even if inviting the facilitator was the administrator's idea. Facilitation invigorates teachers; they may start to make waves. In Soledad and in Pasadena, teachers rebelled against administrative decisions. In Palo Alto several teachers left the centers they were working for, having realized—with a facilitator's help—that the fit wasn't a good one, thus leaving administrators with yet another hiring to do.

It is important that administrators acknowledge their power and be able to exercise it. It is important that facilitators acknowledge their position outside the power structure and be free of the need to engage in power struggles. It is important that both recognize the useful balance between fixing up and facilitation, and learn to collaborate in making use of both strategies at appropriate times and places. There is real potential for mutual learning in this relationship if both parties are open to learning.

Administrators are often isolated because they are in charge (Stine, 1983, p. 81). A facilitator from outside the system has the potential for becoming a peer; participation in a partnership may provide an administrator with others to talk to and/or to delegate some responsibilities to. In Pasadena partnership staff took increasing responsibility for planning and implementing district in-services, as trust was gradually established. The facilitator needs to resist being co-opted by administrators on one hand and by teachers on the other, while remaining accessible to both.

A facilitator who is able over time to gain the trust of both teachers and administrators may become something of an ombudsperson, a mediator between sometimes-opposing interests—on her own initiative or by request. She can tell affirming stories to administrators about teachers *and* to teachers about administrators. Collectively structured partnerships will work only if the facilitator has respect for both teachers and administrators. Individual-oriented partnerships, which bypass system constraints to work only with teachers, need not meet this requirement, but they have less potential for influencing system change.

System constraints on facilitation models

A facilitation model is relatively easy to implement with autonomous, confident, privileged teachers accustomed to making educational choices for themselves and successfully asserting themselves in the face of institutional authority. This description is somewhat more likely, given unequal distribution of power in society, to fit elementary teachers than child care workers, college graduates than persons who barely got through high school, Anglo-Americans than people of color, upper-middle-class than working-class folks, and men rather than women (although most participants in these early childhood education projects were, as would be expected, female). The great majority of all teachers of children, however, are treated as less-than-autonomous professionals in the systems in which they work (Donmoyer, 1981; Kamii, 1985).

Because people oppressed by gender, race, language, and social-class bias have significantly limited experience in making successful choices on behalf of their personal and professional growth, they are unlikely to be trusted, by institutions or by themselves, to make autonomous decisions as classroom teachers, so they are given training rather than practice in critical thinking. They are treated as silent receivers of knowledge (Belenky, Clinchy, Goldberger, & Tarule, 1986), as objects

Implications for Career Development in Early Childhood Education

Some of the staff with whom facilitators worked in these projects were college-graduate, credentialed teachers accustomed to thinking of themselves as smart—comfortable around schools, books, and people who teach in universities. Others had no more than a high school diploma or GED, spoke English as a less-than-comfortable second language, and had long experience with school failure. Facilitators chose to regard *all* of these teachers, regardless of background, as competent learners capable of growth in reflection on practice, in making connections between theory and practice, and in communicating their knowledge to others.

In this book we have taken the position that all early childhood teachers with baseline competence (i.e., the ability to provide a group of children with learning experiences that are developmentally more beneficial than harmful) can be empowered as professionals by facilitation that builds directly on their strengths and assumes their capacity for critical thinking. The more commonly held view is that only elite teacher populations (often, those who are most like teacher educators) are ready for genuine reflection and dialogue—co-learning with a facilitator—and that what the rest need is training, which emphasizes the expertise of the trainer, delivered through telling. This view as applied to children can be found in those schools where only "gifted" children (typically defined by test scores) receive teaching for critical thinking, while the rest (especially those in special education) experience the sort of teaching described by one observant seven-year-old as "They find out what you can't do and they make you do it and do it and do it"—usually on worksheets. For many adults this has been their only experience of school. They were not empowered by it.

The current national debate in early childhood education on educational requirements for teaching staff has generated discussion of a "career lattice" (Bredekamp & Willer, 1992). On such a lattice there is room for the recruitment of liberal arts college graduates into teaching in order to give children exposure to the "brightest and best" (using the narrowly defined academic criteria of some advocates). There is, as well, room for the recruitment of caring community members who share the culture of the parents and children with whom they work and offer excellent adult role models through whom a strong self-concept and significant knowledge can be built. We believe that children need connection with adults from varied backgrounds and that adults' varied backgrounds need full recognition in early childhood education.

An effective career lattice would enable staff entering the field through the community route to earn degree credit for reflection on their experience, rather than have it unacknowledged by college "gatekeepers" to the profession. Conventional training, designed to remedy deficiencies rather than to acknowledge strengths, is too much like the schooling with which many staff have had negative previous experience. Facilitation, in contrast, offers intellectual challenge *connected to teachers' classroom competence* and thus has potential for tapping intellectual competence left untapped by traditional schooling. Breaking the cycle of school failure requires co-learning, as David Beers has described the process in Chapter 1, with teachers listening to learners as well as vice versa. An early childhood education career lattice implies changes in higher education, involving both more interactive teaching modes and more generous transfer of credits earned outside of four-year institutions.

rather than subjects (Freire, 1970; Darder, 1992), to be manipulated for purposes other than their own. Elementary schools are hedged with prescribed textbooks and tests; Head Start, with performance standards. Teachers are thus understandably skeptical of an external facilitator who attempts to affirm and ask rather than critique and tell; so are administrators, who are likely to try to co-opt a facilitator to their own purposes. Institutional purposes are often served by isolating teachers from each other. In many schools teachers are notably reluctant to share ideas with other teachers; the unspoken message is that if you ask for help, you must not know what you're doing. Among teachers, as among children, competition—not cooperation—is the cultural norm. Each teacher's classroom is her own turf (Apelman, 1979). At many schools and centers, faculty/staff meetings are notoriously uninvolving; they are used for announcements, nitty-gritty coordination, and administrators' training agendas. Teachers' own agendas aren't solicited or developed.

Whose agenda is it? is the basic question relevant to teacher empowerment, just as it is in developmentally appropriate practice in early childhood classrooms. Autonomous learners continually generate their own agendas, negotiating them with each other through play during childhood and through dialogue during adulthood. Throughout the stories of these partnerships, teachers' emergent issues partially displaced facilitators' plans for group discussion—appropriately so, because no teacher or group leader can predict in advance all of the significant topics that may emerge. In Palo Alto the facilitator had confidently predicted that mentors' interest would be in new information about children; she was surprised to discover how much time they chose to spend talking about working with other adults, not only their interns, but also their colleagues on the job. In Pasadena both the Play and Language seminar and the Working with Adults seminar, offered in years two and five of the project to interested teachers, jettisoned planned topics on days when teachers' day-to-day complaints spilled over, when teachers were angry about system restructurings, or when children and adults were reacting to recent riots in Los Angeles. By the fifth year of the project, content often emerged in the required in-services as well as in

---

Whose Agenda Is It?

1. Facilitators work with an emergent agenda, leaving room for teachers to move in with their own agendas.

2. Autonomous learners, both adults and children, continually generate their own agendas and negotiate them with peers.

3. Emergent agendas often include issues from outside the classroom that are affecting learners' lives. Empowered learners will expect these issues to be addressed, even at the risk of not covering planned curriculum.

4. Teachers who experience respect for their agendas are more likely to understand the importance of respecting children's play agendas.

> Where wages are inadequate, quality of relationships is insufficient compensation. There is considerable informal evidence, however, that staff turnover decreases in programs where teachers are respected as autonomous thinkers and have opportunities to make significant decisions at both classroom and program levels. Teachers value and often choose to stay at work sites where their growth is supported and their voices are heard.

the smaller, more private seminars, as teachers lost their fears about what might happen if they spoke up.

Teachers and children accustomed to being paid attention to will interrupt training plans and lesson plans with concerns of their own. Empowered, they have less respect for top-down agendas and expect respect for their concerns. Both facilitators and classroom teachers are vulnerable to administrative criticism if they let this happen, but in the best of outcomes, administrators may join the emergent process themselves, taking risks made relatively safe within a context of caring relationships (Noddings, 1984; and see Chapter 4, p. 69 [newsletter], this volume).

Finding and growing facilitators

Facilitation is time consuming; it requires commitment to building relationships with teachers over time. Where can people be found with such time available, with flexibility of hours to match teachers' hours? And what's in it for them if they do?

In the majority of these partnerships, initiative has come from facilitators who, as experienced teachers themselves, wanted to learn—by doing—more about growing teachers. College faculty members, whose responsibilities typically include research and who sometimes have access to funding sources for special projects, are more likely than most other people to have both motivation and flexible schedules. The same may be true of some retired educators.

With relatively limited funding, it is possible to establish a peer-facilitator system like those among community programs in Palo Alto, between Head Start and school-district programs in Pasadena, and among teachers in Boulder. Providing release time for experienced teachers to visit other classrooms and be visited in their own builds a new level of leadership and motivates teachers to stay in the field. Many school districts designate mentor-teachers to give support to new teachers. In some districts one- or two-year teacher-advisor positions are available on a rotating basis to teachers taking a leave from the classroom. Other districts may provide a few longer term positions to specialists who, while working at the district level, are hired as teachers and can return to the classroom in the future.

Organizations such as Renton Vocational Technical Institute, the Australian Kindergarten Union, and teacher centers like Mountain View have employed advisors to work regularly with staff in child care centers and schools while maintaining their independence in relationships with teachers' employers.

As discussed in the introduction to this book, freedom from responsibility for teacher evaluation is probably the single most enabling characteristic of an external facilitator, equalizing in significant respects the relationship between teachers and facilitator. Agency or district personnel whom teachers find trustworthy may be able to function as facilitators—in the role of education coordinator, curriculum consultant, mentor teacher, or head teacher, for example—provided they are outside the evaluation/hiring-and-firing loop.

It is because of their evaluative responsibility that directors are never entirely free to facilitate. However, with tenured or otherwise secure teachers they can come close, and with any staff member a director may choose to practice storytelling, focusing on children and encouraging teachers to do the same (see Carter, Chapter 3).

Making it as a facilitator: Some useful advice

For all facilitators, including administrators trying on the role

1. Become a collector and broadcaster of stories. There are little stories everywhere; you can choose them arbitrarily as long as they're a fair representation. Emphasize stories of children at play, the ultimate focus of attention in an early childhood program.

2. Invite teachers to collect and tell their own stories whenever there's an opportunity—on bulletin boards and in news notes; at staff meetings, parent meetings, in-services, and workshops.

3. Always be generous; give credit whenever possible. Build on strengths.

4. If asked for criticism, don't necessarily give it. Consider whether the criticism will be useful and what you're in fact seeing. Look for points of convergence between your values and the teacher's values. Support her values.

5. If giving advice, couch it as a question to which you genuinely do not know the answer: Would that work? What would happen if you...? Could you try...?

6. Pay attention to teachers' needs hierarchy (Maslow, 1970). Personal problems and job-security issues often take precedence in teachers' lives over events with children in the classroom. Acknowledging and expressing empathy for these priorities is a necessary part of relationship building. It may become part of partnership agenda, as well, when anger becomes a source of energy for collective action.

For facilitators external to the system

7. Pay attention to system realities, especially the constraints under which administrators work. Administrators are the most vulnerable members of the facilitator/teacher/administrator triad; they have the most to lose when things go wrong because they're accountable for things going right. A facilitator's interest in supporting risk taking by teachers needs to be checked out with administrators from time to time. Don't undermine.

8. Respect confidentiality with both teachers and administrators. If you succeed in establishing trust, you'll find out a lot. Passing some of such information along can be useful to everyone only when done in ways that maintain confidentiality.

9. Pay attention to the limits of facilitation; you're a helper, not a rescuer. The agency must establish a baseline for teacher performance, just as teachers must establish limits for children's behavior.

10. Respect and recognize the useful challenge provided by system constraints. Practice the "believing game" (Elbow, 1986) in your dealings with administrators. Be explicit with teachers about how the system works, as you see it, and find out from them how they see it. Strategies for real-world survival, including your own, are part of what you're teaching and learning (Delpit, 1988; Rose, 1989).

Who Might Be a Facilitator?

1. a college faculty member motivated to get out of the ivory tower for a while, who is

a. a subject-matter specialist interested in how people learn her subject, or

b. a teacher educator able to place substantially higher priority on the process of adult learning than on screening teachers for the profession

2. a retired early childhood professional interested in part-time work as consultant or volunteer

3. any consultant interested in building sustained relationships with a small number of teachers rather than in being a "star" for many

4. a peer mentor able to arrange release time for classroom visitation

5. an educational coordinator, trainer, or curriculum specialist, employed by the agency but not responsible for staff evaluation, who has open-ended goals for teacher growth

---

What's In It for the Facilitator?

1. the opportunity to spend time with children in classrooms, with freedom to focus on details

2. the opportunity, for teacher educators, to reconnect with the realities of daily life in classrooms and schools

3. the opportunity to gain greater perspective on the role of the administrator without having to be one

4. the opportunity to build shared-power relationships in which learning is mutual

5. the opportunity to build theory out of practice, collaborating with teachers in data gathering and seeing the direct effects of action research.

Note: Closed-design research not planned in collaboration with teachers does not empower them; instead, it treats them as objects of study, however worthwhile its findings may prove to be. Open-ended ethnographic research in which the researcher is participant-observer has, in contrast, the potential for keeping everyone's agendas in balance, since these agendas are among the data being collected and reflected upon (van Manen, 1990).

Summing up

Facilitation of teacher growth is a second-level model for staff development. Because it offers questions instead of answers, inviting teachers to construct knowledge for themselves with all of the risks inherent in that process, such facilitation relies on a baseline of prior competence established through training— direct teaching of social knowledge about standards for early childhood programs.

Only rules of behavior and names of things are appropriately taught as social knowledge. If you are a student observer, for example, you are expected to sit on a low chair and not interact with the children. If you are a new teaching assistant, you are told this is how we set up snack and this is where we hang children's wet paintings. If you are a teacher in charge of a classroom, you are told these are the licensing regulations for emergency procedures, storage of cleaning materials, and diaper changing, and this is how we expect you to keep lesson plans and to talk with children.

Theory applicable in practice is not social knowledge, although college instructors often teach such theory as if it were. Usable theory is logically constructed by each knower, on the basis of experience and dialogue about experience. Preservice students not in the classroom with children don't need rules for behavior; they need facilitation of their thinking about children and teaching. Adults in the classroom with children, in any role, need rules to begin with—and then facilitation of their thinking about children and teaching.

Effective facilitation depends on personal relationships sustained over time; it isn't a useful model for rapid change in large systems. Because it encourages critical thinking by teachers about all aspects of their work, it represents some risks for those administrators whose security depends on a top-down status quo. It is an open-ended, emergent model, focused on the quality of the learning process rather than on specifiable outcomes. Its objectives, stated behaviorally, are that teachers will reflect on their practice in dialogue with other teachers,

---

Developmentally Appropriate Practice for Adult Learners

Developmentally appropriate practice in early childhood education is also a good model for effective practice in teacher education. Adult learners, like children, need to play—that is, they need to take initiative, make choices among possibilities, act and interact. And, as adults, they need to engage in reflection and dialogue about their experience. They do need baseline social knowledge—training—to get started, to know how to behave, but then they need continuing opportunity to make intellectual and moral judgments, to observe children's behavior, and to put their experience into words that are taken seriously by other adults, both peers and teacher educators. I believe that this process should characterize both college classes and in-service experiences. In both settings, learners should be doing more talking than their instructors do, and their talk should be based in their concrete experience (Jones, 1992).

identify changes they want to try, try them, reflect on them, and continue making changes.

In a presidential address to the American Educational Research Association in 1991, "Managing Dilemmas While Building Professional Communities," Larry Cuban stated,

> What joins together teaching from kindergarten through graduate school is that it is, essentially, uncertain, action driven, ridden with dilemmas, and morally based. . . . Teaching requires making concrete choices among competing values for vulnerable others who lack the teacher's knowledge and skills, who are dependent upon the teacher for access to both, and who will be changed by what the teacher teaches, how it is taught, and who that teacher is. . . . Teachers . . . demonstrate ways of thinking; they model how to inquire and engage others in intellectual exchanges; they disclose how they cope with the inevitable conflicts that arise in classrooms; they display moral virtues. Our character as human beings and how we teach become what we teach. (1992, p. 9)

For teachers of prekindergarten children, there's *deja vu* here; we've been left out again, as we've come to expect in the rhetoric of the American education establishment. But these words describe us too.

In proposing, in this book, a professional growth model for early childhood education, we are making a statement that knowledge about teaching can be constructed by all teachers if they have the opportunity to take their stories seriously. We hope that readers who are directors will be challenged to go beyond training toward a teacher-growth model. As both Carter and Greenough found, in the stories they tell in this book, banking education—the depositing of knowledge (Freire, 1970)—doesn't work; teachers won't consistently implement developmentally appropriate practice unless they have constructed their own understanding of it.

Steve Gravano

That's the slow way, but there isn't any fast way that can be counted on.

We have told stories of programs that tried the longer way around and were rewarded by evident teacher growth both in competence and in the energy that comes from intrinsic motivation. Tapping into the energy of self-directed learning is crucial in promoting quality in schooling and child care. Adults, like children, learn and thrive when they are choosing new experiences for themselves. The trip to the brick factory described by Apelman in Chapter 6 was exciting, but it wasn't just entertainment; elsewhere, Apelman (1981) has commented that the children knew they were going to *learn*, and they liked being learners. As Margaret Mead once said in a keynote address at NAEYC (1973), the "transcendent boredom" of being shut up in classrooms day after day doing the same old things is the worst thing about schools for children and, we would add, for adults; "[it] means that we are taking away from them any kind of chance of responsiveness" (p. 329).

A program director who is interested can try any of several strategies for implementing this model. The simplest may be to invite teachers to find their own resources (college classes, workshops, conferences, and the like), while supporting them with tuition aid, substitute time, and opportunities to share their new ideas with peers. It's important to acknowledge and facilitate the growth of their new ideas, even if these are unrelated to the director's specific goals for a teacher's growth. This model is about valuing growth for its own sake and trusting that it will keep moving along. This individualized strategy leaves it up to teachers to find external facilitators for themselves—in the person of college instructors, teachers' center advisors, or mentors.

In contrast, collective strategies designate facilitators, introduce them to members of a staff, and hope for a good match. Collective models for ongoing partnerships may be implemented within a national structure, such as that provided by CDA advising or by NAEYC accreditation (accreditation could be handled as a planned staff-development process, a genuine self-study with an external facilitator and no pressure to meet a completion deadline); or they may be locally invented, like those in Seattle, Soledad, and Pasadena, with a structure emerging out of the process.

However you choose to go about it, we recommend helping teachers grow.

References

Apelman, M. (1979). An advisor at work. In K. Devaney (Ed.), *Building a teachers' center* (pp. 157–168). San Francisco: Teachers' Center Exchange, Far West Laboratories.

Apelman, M. (1981). *The role of the advisor in the inservice education of elementary school teachers: A case study.* Unpublished doctoral dissertation, University of Colorado, Boulder, CO.

Belenky, M.F., Clinchy, B.M., Goldberger, N.R., & Tarule, J.M. (1986). *Women's ways of knowing: The development of self, voice and mind.* New York: Basic Books.

Bennis, W. (1976). *The unconscious conspiracy: Why leaders can't lead.* New York: AMACOM.

Bredekamp, S., & Willer, B. (1992). Of ladders and lattices, cores and cones: Conceptualizing an early childhood professional development system. *Young Children, 47*(3), 47–53.

Cuban, L. (1992 January–February). Managing dilemmas while building professional communities. *Educational Researcher, 21*(1), 4–11.

Darder, A. (1992). *Culture and power in the classroom.* New York: Bergin and Garvey.

Delpit, L. (1988). The silenced dialogue. *Harvard Educational Review, 58*(3), 280–298.

Donmoyer, R. (1981). The politics of play: Ideological and organizational constraints on the inclusion of play experiences in the school curriculum. *Journal of Research and Development in Education, 14*(3), 11–18.

Elbow, P. (1986). *Embracing contraries: Explorations in teaching and learning.* New York: Oxford University Press.

Freire, P. (1970). *Pedagogy of the oppressed.* New York: Herder and Herder.

Jones, E. (1983). *On the growing edge: Notes by college teachers making changes.* Pasadena, CA: Pacific Oaks College.

Jones, E. (1992, June). *Teaching adults to teach young children.* Paper presented at the first annual conference of NAEYC's National Institute for Early Childhood Professional Development, Los Angeles, CA. (Available from the author)

Kamii, C. (1985). Leading primary education toward excellence: Beyond worksheets and drill. *Young Children, 40*(6), 3–9.

Kleinfeld, J. (1972). *Effective and ineffective teachers of Native high school students.* Fairbanks: University of Alaska, Institute of Social and Economic Research.

Lareau, A. (1989). *Home advantage: Social class and parental intervention in elementary education.* Bristol, PA: Falmer Press.

Maslow, A. (1970). *Motivation and personality.* New York: Harper.

Mead, M. (1973). Can the socialization of children lead to greater acceptance of diversity? *Young Children, 28*(6), 322–329.

Morgan, C. (1983). Journal of a day care administrator. In S. Stine (Ed.), *Administration: A bedside guide* (pp. 11–20). Pasadena, CA: Pacific Oaks College.

Noddings, N. (1984). *Caring: A feminine approach to ethics and moral education.* Berkeley: University of California Press.

Rose, M. (1989). *Lives on the boundary.* New York: Penguin Books.

Stine, S. (1983). *Administration: A bedside guide.* Pasadena, CA: Pacific Oaks College.

van Manen, M. (1990). *Researching lived experience: Human science for an action sensitive pedagogy.* Albany, NY: State University of New York Press.

To contact the author, write Elizabeth Jones, Pacific Oaks College, 5 Westmoreland Place, Pasadena, CA 91103.

Information About NAEYC

NAEYC is...

...a membership-supported organization of people committed to fostering the growth and development of children from birth through age eight. Membership is open to all who share a desire to serve and act on behalf of the needs and rights of young children.

NAEYC provides...

...educational services and resources to adults who work with and for children, including

- *Young Children, the* journal for early childhood educators
- **Books, posters, brochures,** and **videos** to expand your knowledge and commitment to young children, with topics including infants, curriculum, research, discipline, teacher education, and parent involvement
- An **Annual Conference** that brings people from all over the country to share their expertise and advocate on behalf of children and families
- **Week of the Young Child** celebrations sponsored by NAEYC Affiliate Groups across the nation to call public attention to the needs and rights of children and families
- **Insurance plans** for individuals and programs
- **Public affairs information** for knowledgeable advocacy efforts at all levels of government and through the media
- The **National Institute for Early Childhood Professional Development,** providing resources and services to improve professional preparation and development of early childhood educators
- The **National Academy of Early Childhood Programs,** a voluntary accreditation system for high-quality programs for children
- The **Information Service,** a centralized source of information sharing, distribution, and collaboration

For free information about membership, publications, or other NAEYC services...

...call NAEYC at 202–232–8777 or 800–424–2460, or write to NAEYC, 1509 16th Street, N.W., Washington, D.C. 20036–1426.